Personal
POWER

Personal
POWER

• *Use, misuse and abuse* •

Eric Gaudry and Charles D. Spielberger

HarperCollins*Publishers*

Published HarperCollins*Publishers* (Australia) Pty Ltd
22–24 Joseph Street
North Blackburn, Victoria 3130, Australia

Copyright © Eric Gaudry and Charles D. Spielberger 1995
All rights reserved. Except as provided by Australian copyright law, no part of this book may be reproduced without permission in writing from the publisher.

First published 1995
Designed by Rosemarie Franzoni
Cover design by Rosemarie Franzoni
Cover illustration by Charles Blackman, Detail from *From a Midsummer Night's Dream*, 1993, watercolour.

Typeset in HarperCollins*Publishers*, Melbourne
Printed in Australia by Griffin Paperbacks

The National Library of Australia
Cataloguing-in-Publication Data:

Gaudry, Eric.
 Personal power: its use, misuse and abuse.

ISBN 1 86371 447 2.

1. Assertiveness (Psychology). 2. Interpersonal relations.
3. Control (Psychology). I. Spielberger, Charles D. (Charles Donald), 1927– . II. Title

158.2

Contents

1 **The Power to Cope with Life**　　1
2 **Power and Powerlessness**　　6
　　The Abuse of Power
　　The Misuse of Power
　　The Constructive Use of Power
3 **Understanding Anger, Hostility and Aggression**　　26
　　Measuring the Experience, Expression and Control of Anger
　　Risk Factors for Heart Disease
　　Anger and Job Stress
　　Handling Anger Constructively: Personal Power and Relationships
4 **Lowering Our Level of Abuse of Power**　　42
　　How to Lower Your Anger Level
5 **Managing Fear and Anxiety**　　65
　　State and Trait Anxiety
　　Anxiety and Health
　　Anxiety and Education
　　Anxiety in the Workplace
　　Anxiety in Social Situations
　　Anxiety and Relationships
　　Anxiety and Sexual Performance
　　Anxiety in Sports
6 **Lowering Our Levels of Misuse of Power**　　79
　　Regaining Power by Developing Positive Attitudes

7 Power and Self-Esteem   98
    The Concept of Self-Esteem
    The Normative Approach to Measuring Self-Esteem
    The Non-Normative Approach to Measuring Self-Esteem
    Choosing between the Normative and the Non-Normative Approaches
    Characteristics for Good Adjustment and High Self-Esteem

8 Finding Solutions   113
    Step 1: Orientation to the Problem
    Step 2: Defining the Problem
    Step 3: Generation of Options
    Step 4: Selection of the Best Option
    Step 5: Putting the Decision into Action
    Step 6: Assessing the Success of Your Action

9 Being Assertive   135
    Do We Need to Change?
    Can We Change?

10 Using Our Power Constructively   142
    The Signs of a Good Relationship
    Love and Affection

11 Power in Games, Sport and Recreation   171

12 The Use of Power in Industrial Settings   178

13 Power Sharing   189

Appendix 1   192

Appendix 2   207

References   208

chapter 1
The Power to Cope with Life

Each of us has all the power we need to run our life in a sensible way. No one gives us this power; we are born with it. It's ours and no one can take it away from us unless we let them. If we use our power wisely we can make and keep friends and have rewarding and fulfilling relationships. We can also make the most of our skills in our work and our creative life, in games and sport, and have an enjoyable and relaxed social life. In short, our lives can proceed without the fear, anxiety, anger, and depression that beset so many people. Life can be fun!

These claims are not grandiose. All of us have this capacity for happiness and serenity; it is not as difficult to achieve as you might imagine provided you are prepared to keep an open mind and work hard at change. It does mean hard work, however, because it involves change, and many of us see change as threatening.

Change is going on all around us. Each day we grow older. We grow up, find a job, get promoted, change jobs, maybe marry, and sometimes get divorced. We have children. Our financial status changes. Wars begin and end. All of us are involved in a constantly changing environment. Unless we learn to adapt to change, we may feel frustrated, helpless and hopeless, and unable to cope. Some take to drugs like alcohol and tranquillisers for help, while others become angry and lash out verbally or physically.

Yet all along, buried within us is the power, strength, and resourcefulness to cope with whatever life may throw at us. Harnessing this power might be a problem, but it also represents an engrossing challenge. Any system for coping with life has to be broad and general enough to enable us to deal effectively with our personal and family lives, our social lives, our jobs, and our financial affairs. A stable emotional adjustment is essential for coping with life's problems and will contribute to our physical and mental health.

How then do we harness this power? It is clear that many people in our society are not coping well. Their personal relationships are unrewarding and unsatisfying, and many end up in chaos, evident from divorce rates of up to fifty per cent in some Western societies. Many find it difficult to make and keep friends, and have problems mixing socially. Others find their jobs dull, boring or overwhelming, and experience little or no satisfaction in their work.

To harness our personal power we must understand just how much power we have, as well as its limitations. Some of us get into difficulty because we don't realise just how much power we have. Others have problems because they refuse to accept the severe limitations to their ability to deal with their families, colleagues, and people at play and in social settings.

In harnessing your personal power, it is essential to learn the three ways in which power can be used. We have the power to make our own choices. We can use this power constructively by adopting attitudes, beliefs, and ways of behaving that focus on finding solutions to our day-to-day problems so that we can enjoy a calm, relaxed and co-operative way of living. Or we can abuse our power by trying to get our own way all the time, to control and manipulate others and to dominate them and come out on top. Finally, we can misuse our precious power by giving it away to others because we are anxious or fearful, and will do anything to keep the peace. Indeed, some people go to great lengths not to displease or upset others.

Our choice of whether we use our power constructively, or misuse or abuse it, is probably learned very early in life, and is closely linked to our learned emotional responses. Some respond to difficulties and frustrations with hostility, anger, and aggression in one form or another, others with anxiety, worry and fear. A fortunate few remain calm, cool and relaxed. Rather than being overwhelmed by their emotions, they look for solutions, and deal effectively with their problems.

The good news is that no matter how inefficient and ineffective our means of coping have become, and no matter how many years we have been using these methods, change is possible. It is clearly possible to drop one's maladaptive ways, and to replace them with more sensible and effective methods that lead to successful solutions to life's problems.

So, an important goal of this book will be to help you discover and understand the nature of your personal power as well as its limitations. A second goal will be to describe those factors that determine whether a person is likely to use this power wisely, or to abuse or misuse it. The main focus is on how to take control of your emotional life, and to deal more effectively with the environmental and interpersonal factors that influence your emotional responses.

It turns out that the way we use time and, especially, our attitudes towards time, are very important and have far-reaching effects. Individuals who are impatient and display great urgency in getting things done, who often interrupt others' speech, or supply words for them, or push them aside because they are too slow, are often frustrated. Consequently, they are more likely to become angry, hostile and aggressive in their dealings with other people.

The evidence is startlingly clear that these angry people are also very prone to strokes, heart attacks and early death. They have difficulty in their relationships at work and at home, and very high divorce rates. Moreover, they are quite insensitive to accepting that their behaviour is less than ideal and, consequently, are reluctant to change. So, in order to understand why angry, hostile and aggressive people abuse power, we need to look at their attitudes towards time.

Anxious individuals who misuse their power also have a problem with time. They tend to live in the future, always worrying about 'what if'. Because of this apprehension about making mistakes, they tend to procrastinate. They may even become totally immobilised and seemingly incapable of making decisions. When they are pressed to make a decision, they rush in and come to hasty conclusions that often end up in disasters.

Individuals who use their power well are mindful of the past as well as the future, yet they live in the present. They concentrate on what is going on around them *here* and *now*, and on making sensible decisions about how best to deal with present events. For this group, satisfaction and pleasure in life are much greater, and the rate of strokes and heart attacks is significantly lower than for those who are often angry or anxious.

Our attitude towards time is only one of the many factors that determines our emotional states and, in turn, how we use our power. There are many additional elements that we will describe at length as we proceed. However, because anger and anxiety are crucial elements in determining how we use our power, it is necessary to understand these emotions and how they affect our thoughts and behaviour.

One of the authors has devoted more than three decades to research on clarifying the nature of anger, hostility and aggression on the one hand, and of fear, anxiety and nervousness on the other. Based on this research, anger and anxiety are discussed in considerable detail. The authors believe that insight into the frequency and intensity of our own levels of these emotions, how they affect us in our day-to-day lives, and how we respond with anger and anxiety in specific situations is essential for well-being and effective coping with life's problems.

Our experience is that most people are not fully aware of their own emotional life. Therefore, we have included some brief questionnaires that we will ask you to complete and score from time to time. Becoming aware of the extent of your anger and anxiety is an important first step in providing a more meaningful understanding of the changes to make in order to maximise control of your own life in ways you and others will find rewarding. The interpretation of your scores will be included in the directions. These interpretations are based on the assessment of many thousands of men and women under various conditions.

Let us turn now to a fuller and more comprehensive description of the nature of personal power, and the ways you can use it constructively, abuse it, or misuse it.

chapter 2
Power and Powerlessness

To use your personal power effectively, it is essential for you to understand its nature and how to make it work for you. Here are the three major assumptions on which our analysis of personal power is based:

1. We *all* have the power to run our lives in a sensible way.
2. We have *no* legitimate power to run the life of any other person.
3. No one possesses the power to run his/her life sensibly on all occasions. We are not perfect! Our power is imperfect!

The word 'all' in the statement of the first assumption emphasises that it applies to everyone regardless of gender, race, family background or previous experience. It applies to individuals from more or less trouble-free backgrounds, as well as to those whose childhood included mental or physical brutality, rape, incest, or any other form of physical or emotional trauma. Anyone can change; we can all rise above our backgrounds and learn to run our lives in a sensible way.

The word 'sensible' is used quite deliberately in stating our initial assumption. It means 'in a way dictated by common sense'; 'sensible' is not necessarily equated with 'logical'. For example, Sandra is having an affair with John who introduces her to his best friend, Bruce. Bruce and Sandra fall in love and marry. A few months later they decide to have a party and Sandra suggests inviting John. Bruce says no, but Sandra insists that her affair with John is long over and that it is not 'logical' to leave him off the guest list. So John is invited. At the party Bruce sees John with his arm around Sandra. He becomes furious and starts an angry scene. The question here is not whether it was *logical* to have invited John but whether it was *sensible*. In this case, the invitation probably did not make good sense even though it was logical.

The second assumption restricts personal power to running one's own life; there is no legitimate basis for using our power to control the life of another. It is difficult enough for one to manage one's own life without trying to dominate the life of anyone else. Nevertheless, many well-intentioned people tell others, especially those closest to them, such as partners or family members, what they think is best for them. It is not uncommon, for example, for parents to try to influence the relationships or occupations of sons or daughters. Sometimes directly, often more subtly, parents try to take over, manage, and direct the lives of their children. While they truly believe such 'advice' is helping, it often prevents the child from learning how to cope with the world.

It is essential to avoid confusion between rights and responsibilities. While children are young, the responsibilities of parents include keeping them safe from harm, providing unconditional love and affection, and educating them so that they are able to make sensible decisions for themselves. To the extent that parents are successful, their children will become effective, fully functioning adults who are responsible for their own lives, and for their emotional responses and behaviour. Parents have no right to dominate their children any more than they have the right to abuse, bash or otherwise force them to do things that are not sensible or in their children's best interests.

The limitations of personal power become very clear in dealing with others. No one can make a person do something unless that person agrees, or unless physical force is used. To all intents and purposes, we are in charge only of our own lives, and are not responsible for the lives of others.

Unfortunately, when people marry or enter into close relationships, they often believe that they acquire special rights. This is simply *not* true. We cannot *own* a wife or husband, lover, or child. They are responsible for themselves. What we do get in a close relationship is a greater responsibility to share and communicate, to be helpful and kind, and so on. We do not suddenly gain a special right to criticise, put down, dominate or lean on, or even have sex with the other person. Apart from being helpful, kind, and generous, we should encourage those around us to become emotionally independent, and learn to make their own decisions. Once a person recognises that he or she has no legitimate right to manipulate or control anyone else and begins to practise this principle, it is a great relief. When we stop trying to protect, dominate, and control others, we have more time and energy to run our own lives in a sensible way.

The third assumption is especially important because it acknowledges the fact that we are all imperfect people, living in an imperfect world. There is no such thing as the perfect husband, wife, lover, or child. No matter how hard we try, everyone makes mistakes. Occasionally we say the wrong thing or do something silly. This often occurs when we are tired or hungry, or experience some stressful event. Being perfect is simply impossible, so we must be content with doing the best we possibly can.

Accepting and acknowledging our human imperfections allows us to say things such as: 'Sorry, I made a mistake' or 'I should not have said that. Let's start again'. Or we can say 'I don't understand that. Would you explain more clearly what you meant'. Or when overworked or overburdened, 'I need help!' Most of us know very little about astronomy or nuclear physics, or even how to fix a broken refrigerator. But we do have the power to *say* that we don't know, and the power to *ask* for help.

If we accept our own imperfections, we can become less critical of others who are also imperfect. Many people are overly critical of their partners who are not perfect housekeepers or not good at fixing things, or who dress in unconventional ways. Let's accept the fact that we are limited in knowledge and ability in many areas, which makes us mistake-prone and fallible and thus entitled to act in less-than-perfect ways. But so is everyone else with whom we come into contact. Of course, this does not mean that we must condone behaviour that is rude, dangerous, or otherwise unacceptable. It *does* mean that we need to give up demanding perfection in ourselves and in others.

Let us now turn to a description of how men and women actually use their power. There are, in fact, three general ways of using power. We can abuse it, misuse it, or use it constructively. Although some of us may prefer a particular way of coping with life, for example by abusing our power and rarely using other methods, most people use all three approaches, switching from one to the other from time to time. Our ultimate goal is, of course, to change so that we can use our power constructively while abandoning the other two strategies.

The Abuse of Power

Abuse of power occurs when we become aggressive and try to impose our will on others, or try to manipulate and control them. We may do this in a number of ways, some of which are listed in Table 2.1.

The first column lists behaviours that are commonly seen as aggressive. These include punching, shouting, demanding, and threatening.

Column 2 lists behaviours that are not so readily interpreted. Putting someone down by being sarcastic, by ignoring them, or by being overly critical are clear examples of verbal aggression. But so is shutting someone out of your life. For example, consider a middle-aged couple whose grown children have recently moved out. When the parents are alone they get along very well, communicate clearly, and share their lives. However, when the couple is visited by their children the wife completely ignores her husband, talking only with the children. This, too, is aggressive behaviour even though it may not be recognised as such.

Table 2.1 Forms of aggression

being intolerant	giving silent treatment
being overly possessive	manipulating
being racist	ignoring
being sexist	pushing
being sulky	putting down
being vengeful	shoving
blackmailing	coercing
punishing	shutting out
shouting	being overly critical
punching	being sarcastic
demanding	withholding praise, sex, information
forcing	controlling
threatening	

Racism and sexism also involve aggressive behaviours, and sulking is an aggressive means of punishing someone or trying to get our own way. Sarcasm, which may be humorous, is usually presented as a sort of joke, but it is not funny to the target of the joke. Rather, sarcasm is generally designed to hurt, with the sting incorporated in telling the story: 'So you are going to open a boutique. Well, Christian Dior had better watch out.'

The motive behind aggression is often to take someone's power from them in order to bend them to our will, or to get them to agree with us. Aggressive people see life as a place where the object is to win, to get their own way at all costs. Unfortunately, many children are brought up with this combative view of life, which is often reinforced by teachers and peers. Consequently, despite the fact that most humans choose to live in groups, individuals compete with one another in a state that often resembles warfare. Their aim in life is to dominate, to get their own way, regardless of the rights and feelings of those with whom they interact, whether at home, at work, or in social or sporting activities.

Being competitive, of course, is not necessarily bad. Indeed, the object in games, sports, and business is to succeed. The problem with competitiveness arises from overly aggressive and selfish attitudes, for example: 'Unless I win, I am a failure'; 'Coming in second is not acceptable; I *have* to win'. We often see such feelings displayed when playing games like Scrabble. Suppose two people are playing. The game is nearly over and one is clearly ahead. Suddenly the opponent scores over 50 points, and achieves an unbeatable lead. At this change of fortune, the loser throws down the tiles, upsets the board, and refuses to finish the game. She is combative and *must* win at any cost. Being overly combative and having to win reflect abusive power needs.

The maladaptive effects of angry, aggressive behaviour are well documented. Since no one wants to be on the receiving end of aggression, one major effect of such behaviour is to alienate the receiver. Angry, aggressive behaviour creates a distance between people, pushes them apart, and may even result in an unbridgeable gap. Simply put, it destroys relationships. Thus, a second major effect of inappropriate aggressive behaviour is the alienation of those who are unfortunate enough to receive or even witness such actions.

Suppose two children are witnessing a violent argument between their parents. As the battle rages, these children, who need unconditional love and affection in order to feel secure and to grow emotionally, are likely to be devastated. Similarly, few people at a dinner party enjoy witnessing a couple brawling about the woman's lack of housekeeping skills or the man's excessive drinking at social gatherings. As a rule, no one, young or old, likes being involved as a witness to the arguments and difficulties of others. Observers as well as those on the receiving end of aggression are damaged by such behaviour.

A third negative effect of angry, aggressive behaviour is that it blocks or interferes with communication by 'building a wall' between people. Although words can permeate this barrier, once the participants become engaged in an argument they stop listening, adopt rigid and often extreme positions, and become increasingly inflexible. Getting their own way is all that matters. During such encounters, angry people are apt to say and do stupid things. Quite often, an angry encounter results in individuals not speaking to one another for some time after the argument ends. This failure to communicate may last for an hour, a week, or, in some cases, for a lifetime!

Feelings of guilt about hurtful things said and done during arguments often result from angry, aggressive behaviour. Like anger, guilt frequently provokes people to do stupid things, thus compounding the impact of aggression and bringing about further harm. Guilt can continue to be an extremely harmful emotion unless and until it is removed by a person making amends for the harm that he or she has caused.

Listing the effects of angry and aggressive behaviour shows just how damaging these emotions can be. They can result in:
- saying and doing stupid things
- alienation of the recipient of such behaviour
- alienation of those witnessing aggression
- breakdown in communication between the persons involved
- feelings of guilt by both parties to an argument

Of course, if you are big enough, strong enough, clever enough, or have a loud enough voice, you *can* force others to agree with you, or to comply and go along with your demands. But the list of possible effects suggests that the price one pays is very high, especially in the long run. Many homes are full of unhappy, frightened people; the divorce courts do a roaring trade, the criminal courts are full of people charged with assault and worse; and the workplace is a scene of resentment for those forced to do things by someone who behaved aggressively.

In angry, aggressive, and hostile behaviour, the self is generally the major focus of interest. The concern is all about 'I' and 'me' and 'my' rights and needs.

'How dare you say that to *me*. I won't put up with it.'

'Don't criticise *me*. I will not stand for it.'

'You have no right to speak to *me* like that.'

At this point, we note that there are hundreds of words and phrases in the English language that describe individuals when they are angry. Some, such as 'annoyed', 'furious' and 'enraged', are obvious synonyms for more or less intense angry feelings. Others, such as 'being sarcastic' or 'resentful', are less obvious, but certainly have a large anger component. If the motive is to force another to agree, if it's about getting one's own way, or if the behaviour is designed to hurt someone else, then anger and aggression are usually involved.

Table 2.2 lists a number of words that are used to describe people when they are angry, or where anger is an important component of an emotional state.

The first column consists of commonly accepted words for describing ourselves or others in an active state of anger.

The second column contains words that reflect less direct (passive-aggressive) or suppressed expressions of anger.

Table 2.2 Emotional states with anger components

Active states	*Passive states*	*Depressive states*
annoyed	bitter	ashamed
disgusted	boiling	bored
enraged	brooding	dejected
frustrated	envious	depressed
full of hate	giving silent treatment	full of self-pity
furious	jealous	guilty
indignant	morose	lonely
intolerant	smouldering	
irritated		
resentful	sulking	
sarcastic	sullen	
vengeful		

The words in the third column of Table 2.2 describe depressive states, where anger is turned inwards against the self. Although the feelings described in column three are not often seen as indicating anger, if we analyse the way most people get depressed, the anger component becomes clearer.

Take the case of a man, definitely not the handyman type, with a problem changing the wheel on his car. He finally mastered this art, but then bought a new car where, unlike the old one, the hubcaps were held on by the heads of the wheel bolts. When he had to replace a flat tyre on the new car, he did all the things he had previously learned — placing the hubcap on the ground, and then the bolts inside so they wouldn't get lost, and finally replacing the wheel and tightening the bolts to hold the wheel in place. At this stage he discovered he had a piece left over — the hubcap. The old method of replacing the wheel didn't work. With the third flat tyre in about a year he became furious, shouted, carried on, and jumped on the hubcap, destroying its shape. For the rest of the day he felt depressed.

The dynamics of this man's depression are shown in Figure 2.1. As may be noted, depression is a four-stage process, involving a lot of anger.

Stage One: We make a mess of whatever we are doing.
Stage Two: We get angry with the object. '*Stupid* car, *stupid* design, *stupid* hubcap.' (Jumps on hubcap.)
Stage Three: We get angry with ourselves. '*I've* done it again. *I've* messed it up. *I've* failed. *I am* a failure.'
Stage Four: Feelings of depression. '*I'm* hopeless. *I'm* no good.'

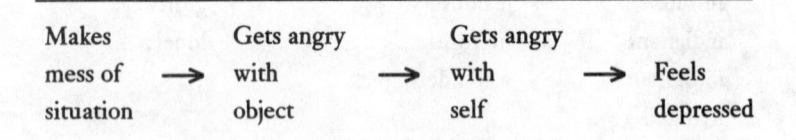

| Makes mess of situation | → | Gets angry with object | → | Gets angry with self | → | Feels depressed |

Figure 2.1 The development of depression

As will become clearer when we consider anger management in a later chapter, we must look at the underlying feelings of anger that we have developed over the years in response to frustrating situations. As far as anger and hostility are concerned, our Scrabble player may have developed attitudes and beliefs that predisposed her to display high levels of aggression in a wide variety of situations. These attitudes and beliefs may reflect a low level of self-esteem and underlying feelings of insecurity. The following lists of beliefs are often at the root of such feelings:

1. It is vitally important to win.
2. Winning makes me feel good and proves I am superior.
3. When I win, it proves that I'm *not* inferior.
4. It is catastrophic to lose.
5. If I lose, it means that I am inferior.
6. To lose is to fail. Therefore, to lose proves that I am a failure.
7. It would be dreadful if others saw me lose.
8. It doesn't matter if others get hurt as long as I win.
9. It's OK to make excuses and to blame others when I lose or when I fail.

Such underlying attitudes and feelings often motivate acts of aggression aimed at damaging, hurting, destroying or punishing some object or person.

The Misuse of Power

We misuse power by giving it away. This is frequently associated with a state of anxiety. Anxious people need approval from others and are often labelled 'people-pleasers'. In situations where they believe that someone will disapprove of their behaviour, or where they are afraid they will be rejected, or fail to please, anxiety will surge. The symptoms of anxiety are very unpleasant and sometimes intensely painful. They may include trembling of the hands and legs, 'butterflies' in the stomach, sweaty hands, dry mouth and lips, rapid heart rate, elevated blood pressure, and very tense muscles. Above all, there is a terrible feeling of something about to go wrong, of apprehension and dread.

Certain situations frequently evoke anxiety responses and, indeed, sometimes panic — a very high level of anxiety. Among these are taking an examination, acting (stage fright), making a speech in public or at a social function, and appearing on television. Many, if not most, people feel an increase in anxiety when they are being evaluated or just before performing. Indeed, anxiety reactions can be so intense that one's mind 'goes blank'. Such reactions result from fear of failure or rejection, or being judged by others to be an idiot or a fool. Consequently, many people go to extreme lengths to avoid exposure to situations and events where there is a potential for negative evaluation. Others go ahead but perform at a level far below that of which they are capable.

Consider a young man at a dance who sees an attractive young woman sitting alone. He is attracted to her and wants to ask her to dance. So he begins to walk toward her, rapidly at first, then slows down, and eventually stops a few metres away from her. He looks wistfully at her, but then returns to his starting point. His problem was that he was running a tape in his head where he saw himself asking the young woman to dance and she said 'Get lost. You'd be the last one I'd dance with'. High anxiety caused by a strong fear of rejection stopped him dead in his tracks.

Another situation that seems to lead to increased anxiety is asking the boss for a raise. Consider the reactions of an underpaid secretary who decided after much soul-searching to ask for a salary rise. Each evening when she came home from work her partner asked her what had happened, and each time she came up with an excuse for her procrastination:

- Well, I thought I'd wait because she was busy with visitors.
- I couldn't do it today; things are so hectic the day before pay-day.
- I spent the whole day with one of my clients, and wasn't in the office.

Anxious people can find endless excuses to justify their lack of action, which can put an enormous strain on their relationships with family and friends. What do the anxiety-provoking situations listed below have in common?

- making a speech in public
- going to a social gathering where you don't know the other guests
- asking a stranger to dance with you
- asking the boss for an increase in pay

If we can identify the common elements in these situations, we will be better able to understand anxiety, and thus do something about our own misuse of power that results from intense anxiety.

The most obvious thing about these four events is that they all involve other people. In the example of the young woman who was afraid to ask her boss for a salary increase, as she thought about it she imagined that she would be rejected. This attitude was a crucial factor in determining her anxiety level, and ultimately, her procrastination. The main factor that causes anxiety seems to be how we react to people who might judge us. If we consider their reactions to our asking for a rise, our request for a dance, our speech, as very important or necessary for our well-being, then anxiety becomes a problem.

On the other hand, we may say to ourselves something like: 'Well, I'll give it a go. I'll give it my best shot. It will be good if it works out, but if I don't succeed it is not the end of the world. It is my behaviour, my actions, my words that are not working. I am not being rejected as a person. I am not a failure. To fail at something does not mean *I* am a failure!' To clarify this point, suppose the young man does ask the young woman to dance and she says no. She may have refused because she had promised to dance with someone else, was tired or not feeling well, was ready to go home, or for any number of reasons. She rejected the request, but not necessarily the person. Unfortunately, anxious people may think: 'Well, that was a disaster! She doesn't like me. I've failed again. I'm hopeless'.

The anxious young man who did not take the risk of asking the young woman to dance had come to the conclusion that she would reject him if he did. From our perspective, he exhibited selfish, self-centred behaviour. He had two ideas in his head: (1) 'I like you'; and (2) 'I want to dance with you'. By depriving her of this information, he gave her no opportunity to accept or refuse his request. This is selfish, self-centred and potentially maladaptive behaviour. It is also reasonable to assume that the procrastinating secretary won't ask for a pay rise because she plays negative tapes in her mind. She sees her boss responding: 'A rise? There's no way in the world I would recommend you for an increase.'

Finally, the speech-maker thinks: 'I'm not good at this sort of thing. My mind will go blank; they will think I'm a fool, or maybe they'll all start talking and laughing and perhaps even get up and walk out!' Thus, some of the features that these situations have in common for anxious people include:

1. the involvement of at least one other person
2. the possibility of rejection by another person or group of people
3. the possibility of failure and/or being seen by others to fail
4. imagined scenarios that include failure or rejection
5. apprehension about the future in each scenario
6. the probability that other persons will judge us negatively
7. approval from others being sought in a dependent way
8. self as the focus of attention

A major defining characteristic of anxious people is that they respond to threatening situations by imagining failure or rejection, where the imagined future becomes the present reality; i.e. failure and rejection seem to have already occurred.

Many anxious people are perfectionists in certain aspects of their behaviour. Such perfectionism is designed to avoid criticism. The perfectionist housewife whose home is so clean you could eat off the floor does not simply have high standards; her behaviour is a pathological defence against possible criticism. It is a product of anxiety. When our lives are so dependent on the approval of others that we try to become perfect in order to please them, we hand our power over to these others, allowing fear of their disapproval to shape our lives.

Another common people-pleasing response is to say 'yes' when we really mean 'no'. The following examples demonstrate the chaos that this type of behaviour can cause. Let us consider, for example, a married couple where the husband suggests sex. The wife doesn't feel like sex, but she says yes. Because she doesn't want sex at this time, she probably won't enjoy it. So the husband probably won't enjoy it, and when it's all over they might have a row. A fine example of how to please another person!

A second example is that of a designer who says yes to a request to do something 'that will only take half a minute', yes when asked to 'do this little job', and yes to other similar requests. The result is a studio so piled up with work that it can't possibly be completed in less than a month. The designer becomes even more anxious because she can't complete the work, and others whose demands are not being met become angry because their work isn't being done. People-pleasing at work again!

Procrastination is also a self-defeating characteristic of anxious people. This was illustrated by the secretary who kept putting off asking for a pay rise. The worst form of procrastination is to become so immobilised that no action is taken.

The Constructive Use of Power

We have seen that some people often believe the most important thing in life is the approval of others. These people-pleasers put their own well-being in the hands of others. If another person says 'Well done', or 'Gee, you're clever', they feel marvellous. On the other hand, if they are told 'You're wrong', 'You've made a mistake', or 'I don't agree with you', their world falls apart.

In some ways, anxious people are like young children; they are emotionally dependent on others for their existence, i.e. 'I am what you say I am', or even 'I am what I think you think I am'. Anxious people misuse their power by handing it over to others. Hostile, angry, aggressive people believe that the most important thing in life is winning and getting their own way. They *abuse* their power by taking — or trying to take — power away from others, by making them dependent, and by dominating them. Such forcing, threatening, bullying and coercing has disastrous consequences.

If life is not about pleasing others, and it is not about winning, what philosophy *can* we use to guide us in our daily affairs? The one that works best for most people is *Life is about doing the best we can with whatever skill, personality, and ability we possess. It is about trying to make sensible decisions and putting these decisions into practice.*

Not only will we benefit by changing our thoughts as to what life is really all about, but we may also need to modify the emotional state that governs our minute-to-minute dealings with the environment where we live, work and play.

We need to learn to *keep calm* or *become calm*, in order to think clearly and maximise the chances of making good decisions. Keeping calm may require a change of focus. As previously noted, the focus of interest for anxious, submissive people, and for angry, aggressive people, is the *self*. In contrast, those who use their power constructively have a different focus. These people say things such as:

- 'What's the sensible thing to do here?'
- 'What's the best way to fix this?'
- 'Which option is most likely to work?'

The focus of interest is external, not inside the person. It is directed towards the situation to be dealt with, the problem that has arisen, the choice that needs to be made.

The behaviour that arises from a calm appraisal of a situation, based on examining the available options, is *assertion*. Assertive people try to remain calm rather than becoming angry or anxious. But when they get angry, they try to cool down and get rid of the anger as quickly as possible. They use anger constructively as a danger signal, i.e. as a warning that something is wrong, needs fixing, or has to be thought through, so they calm down and fix it.

Assertive people accept their limitations, recognise that everyone is mistake-prone and not infallible, and work on communicating with others to improve their knowledge, and thus their decision-making. They have learned to be honest, tolerant and direct, and are open and willing to learn. The opposite of open is closed and secretive.

While the reasons for being closed and secretive vary, one major reason seems to stem from feeling different from, and not measuring up to, societal norms. Thus, a woman who is a poor cook and who loathes housework may have a poor self-image because she accepts the stereotype that 'all women should be good cooks and housewives'. Instead of accepting reality, she may become defensive and lie about the fact that her husband does the major part of both activities.

Introverted and shy men often pretend to be extroverted and the life of the party because they believe that being introverted is somehow second-class. The evidence, of course, is that introverted men and women who accept this in themselves are just as successful and happy in every area of life as those who are extroverted. Trying to be an extrovert when you are an introvert is living a lie; it is a recipe for anxiety and disaster.

This tendency to conform will be discussed more fully later, in the context of the productive use of power. Assertive people appear to have accepted themselves, warts and all, and do not feel compelled to conform because of anxiety. They have no use for secrecy about themselves, especially in regard to any emotional problems they may experience from time to time. Instead they ask for help, discuss their emotional problems, and try to resolve their difficulties. Since they are open, not closed, they communicate better, and thus they make good use of their personal power.

Assertive people protect their rights and feelings, and while they don't let others push them around or trample on them, they are tolerant. Rather than being arrogant, they accept the rights of others to be different — to have different ideas and different attitudes and value systems. They realise that many older people have a great deal of wisdom, while the very young are often able to get at the heart of a problem because they possess insights adults may have lost.

A major motive of assertive people is to communicate. In their search for sensible decisions, they tolerate differences in outlook, status, and circumstance. Neither race, skin colour, age nor gender is seen as a barrier to communication. But assertive men and women do not tolerate unacceptable behaviour because that would not be sensible. Tolerance, as used here, however, does not mean putting up with offensive behaviour: that would be stupid.

Another characteristic of the assertive individual is directness, rather than being indirect or hinting at what you mean. The following are two examples of ineffective behaviour based on indirect methods of communication. The first is a young couple who both work a five-day week. Since the husband usually gets home earlier, he has agreed to cook the evening meal during the week while the wife cooks on weekends. On this particular day he had a rough time at work and feels emotionally and physically drained. He wants help preparing dinner, so he speaks to his wife when she gets home. The conversation goes something like this:

Husband: I had a rough day at work today. Three people were out sick and there was a deadline to meet. It was frantic.

Wife: Sorry to hear that, but it happens in all business.

Husband: Well, I'm really worn out.

Wife: As soon as you've cooked the dinner, you should go to bed and relax.

He is hinting that he would like help; he doesn't ask for it. This leads to misunderstanding and probably results in frustration and annoyance on his part. An assertive way of handling the situation would be:

Husband: I've had a rough day at work and I'm really tired. I know it's not your night for cooking the dinner, but I would really appreciate some help in the kitchen. Will you come now please?

Of course this might not work, but it is a direct statement of his feelings and expectations and dramatically increases the chance of getting the help he wants.

Willingness to learn is an important feature of assertive behaviour. It implies acceptance of the proposition that no one is infallible or perfect. Realising this, assertive people will say and do things where they can be wrong. Rather than getting upset with errors, they try to learn from them. An example might be:

Boss: I've just read this letter you typed and I think you spelled commitment wrongly. It should have two t's.

Secretary: I'm fairly sure it has one but let's look it up (finds word in dictionary). Look here (points). One t.

Boss: OK. You're right. My mistake. At least I've learned something today.

In this case, both the boss and the secretary are assertive. Each calmly concentrates on the problem and its solution. Neither is concerned with proving a point, self-justification, or pleasing the other. This is good, clear communication.

The way in which people relate to one another, their 'relationship style', also varies. Submissive people are basically dependent, aggressive people see life as an area of combat and competition, and assertive people view life as a co-operative endeavour based on communication. Table 2.3 is a summary of some of this chapter and highlights differences in the way these three groups approach and deal with their lives.

Those who abuse and misuse personal power generally find life difficult. They have relationship problems as well as social difficulties. Both are likely to use alcohol and tranquillisers in excess with a fairly high risk of addiction. In addition, both are at risk from elevated blood pressure and from strokes and heart attacks.

In contrast, those who remain calm find life much easier. They enjoy social functions and new experiences because change is not threatening. They easily admit mistakes and concentrate on solutions to the problems and issues confronting them. This, in turn, leads to a high degree of success.

Obviously, learning to use power productively is not an easy task. Not only must we question our value system and lifetime collection of attitudes, but we also have to come to terms with the paradoxical nature of what we will find during this questioning.

1. The more we try to please others, the less we please them, and the more chaotic our life becomes. The more we seek approval from others, the less they approve of us.
2. The more we try to win, the more we lose, and the more chaotic our life becomes.

Table 2.3 The three faces of power

	Abuse	*Misuse*	*Constructive Use*
Motive	win at all costs; get own way; dominate	gain approval; avoid censure; please others	find solutions; do best you can; communicate
Time	live in past; fast tempo	live in future	live in present; relaxed tempo
Focus	self	self	the issue
Emotion	anger	anxiety	calmness
Attitude	hostile	fearful	friendly
Behaviour	aggressive	submissive	assertive
Relationship style	combative	dependent	co-operative
Decision-making style	snap decisions; rigid defence even if wrong	avoidance; hesitation or impetuous choice	scrutiny of options; change if wrong
Reaction to mistakes	anger; blame someone else; sulk	panic; flight	admit mistake; try to fix; ask for help
Attitude to change	inflexible; rigid	fearful	open to change
Attitude to self	overvalue self	undervalue	realistic acceptance
Conformity	conforms to values of similar people	highly conformist	non-conformist; do what is sensible
Use of drugs and alcohol	high	very high	little or no use
Attitude to authority	resentful	submissive	accepting
End result	chaos	chaos	finds life easy

3 The more we accept the limitations of our power, the higher our level of achievement.

In the next few chapters we will discuss how to change by presenting evidence from experimental, clinical, and medical studies, which demonstrate not only that change is possible, but that it has significantly improved the lives of those who made the effort to alter their ways. Why hang on to inefficient, ineffective, and ultimately deadly ways of living when, with a little effort, you can begin to enjoy life to its fullest and experience touches of serenity and peace?

The next chapter looks at anger, hostility, and aggression in great detail and concentrates on managing these factors. Before you start, turn to Appendix 1 on page 192 and follow the directions for completing and scoring the three questionnaires:

1 Self-Analysis Questionnaire STPI Form X–1
2 Self-Analysis Questionnaire STPI Form X–2
3 Anger Expression (AX) Scale

Both the Self-Analysis Questionnaires have twenty items. The AX Scale contains twenty-four items. When you have completed the three scales you will be shown how to score them and tables will be provided to enable you to interpret your own scores.

chapter 3
Understanding Anger, Hostility and Aggression

Although psychologists have long been aware of the impact of anger, hostility, and aggression on our day-to-day lives, it is only recently that these concepts have been carefully and fully analysed, leading to the development of standard measures of anger. After more than a decade of research, Spielberger and his co-workers have produced scales that are used worldwide to reliably measure the experience, expression and control of anger. The large database on which these scales were developed permits a meaningful comparison of the anger level of a particular individual with those of the average person. The three tests you have just completed are based on results of this research.

When Spielberger first began his research, he became aware of the need to clarify the confusion regarding the interchangeable use of the terms *a*nger, *h*ostility, and *a*ggression, which he refers to collectively as the AHA! Syndrome. While the three terms are closely related, there are important conceptual differences in their connotations. To highlight these differences, Spielberger has proposed the following working definitions of anger, hostility, and aggression

> *Anger* refers to an emotional state consisting of *feelings* that vary in intensity from mild irritation or annoyance to intense fury and rage.

Hostility usually involves angry feelings, but this concept also has the connotation of a complex set of *attitudes* and *beliefs* that motivate aggressive behaviours. Hostile persons are often mean, vicious, vindictive and cynical.

While anger and hostility refer to feelings and attitudes, the concept of *aggression* generally implies destructive or punitive *behaviour* directed towards damaging or destroying objects, or injuring other people.

Thus, anger refers to feelings, hostility is related to attitudes and beliefs that are motivated by anger, and aggression describes the actual destructive behaviours that are often displayed by an angry person. Since hostility and aggression are usually motivated by angry feelings, anger is at the core of the AHA! Syndrome. While angry feelings are invariably accompanied by activation (arousal) of the autonomic nervous system, it is the unique experiential quality and intensity of these feelings that best defines the emotion of anger.

Measuring the Experience, Expression and Control of Anger

Spielberger's next contribution to the theory of anger was in recognising the need to distinguish between the intensity of angry feelings at any given time, and how often anger is experienced. The section of the completed questionnaire that we labelled as State-Anger asked you to indicate how angry you feel *right now, at this moment*. This scale measures the intensity of your angry feelings, which Spielberger calls 'state-anger' (S-Anger). S-Anger refers to the angry feelings that most of us experience when we are provoked by particular situations, such as being attacked or criticised unfairly.

The section of the questionnaire that asked how you *generally feel* measures how often a person gets angry. This facet of anger, called 'trait-anger' (T-Anger), measures individual differences in anger proneness. A person high in T-Anger is like the man or woman who is described as a 'hothead', or as having an 'explosive temper'. Such persons become angry very easily because they perceive a wide range of situations as annoying, irritating, and frustrating, and tend to respond to such situations with surges of anger. Although a person with high T-Anger experiences S-Anger more often, someone low in T-Anger who is usually calm and placid may also respond with a surge of intense anger if his family is attacked, or her honesty questioned.

If you were to fill in the T-Anger questionnaire at a later date you would probably have a similar score because it requires you to report how you generally feel, and your responses would remain pretty much the same. Thus, T-Anger is considered to be a relatively stable disposition. In contrast, S-Anger can fluctuate markedly, depending on the circumstances. For example, someone who is at home relaxing after work would probably have a low score on the S-Anger scale, whereas the same person would respond quite differently if angered by an insulting telephone call, leading to a high S-Anger score. But this person's T-Anger score would be essentially the same in both situations.

Spielberger has recently distinguished between experiencing angry feelings and the expression of anger, and has developed scales to measure whether anger is held in or let out. Because feeling and expressing anger are closely related, in order to measure anger expression one must examine how people react or behave when they feel angry. In the third part of the questionnaire you have just taken, anger expression was distinguished from angry feelings by your being asked to indicate how you react or behave 'when you feel angry or furious'. In other words, what do you actually do when you feel angry? Since most people try, at least to some extent, to control their angry feelings, this questionnaire also included items designed to evaluate the extent to which people try to control their anger.

Questionnaire items indicating the likelihood of expressing anger openly and outwardly when one feels angry or furious include: 'I make sarcastic remarks to others', 'I say nasty things', and 'If someone annoys me, I'm apt to tell him or her how I feel'. Items indicating a tendency to experience and suppress anger, rather than expressing it, include: 'I'm irritated a great deal more than people are aware of', and 'I boil inside but don't show it'. Examples of items that assess anger control are: 'I keep my cool',

'I control my angry feelings', and 'I try to be tolerant and understanding'.

In summary, in order to fully comprehend the nature of anger and its effects on behaviour, it is essential to understand:

1. the difference between anger, hostility, and aggression
2. the difference between state and trait anger
3. the difference between the experience and expression of anger
4. whether anger is held in (suppressed) or let out (expressed)
5. the extent to which one attempts to control angry feelings

Let us now look at the results of several experimental studies that have investigated the effects of anger, hostility, and aggression on various aspects of our lives. We begin with an examination of the relationship between the angry personality and heart attacks.

Risk Factors for Heart Disease

For many generations in folk wisdom a connection has been recognised between anger and death from heart attacks. Even so, it has taken a long time for researchers on coronary heart disease (CHD) to equate the apoplexy of folk wisdom to 'cardiovascular accidents' (strokes) and 'myocardial infarctions' (the most common type of heart attack). Research findings now suggest that such internal disasters might well occur in the wake of frequent bursts of intense fury. This poetic irony, that rage directed at others seems to lash back and strike the heart muscle, cannot be ignored. In everyday life, the anger wasted on trivia, for example in traffic jams and ticket lines, and the 'urge to kill' that boils up so commonly in such situations, are most likely to act on the victim least intended — oneself.

Science is a continuing process. Therefore, a brief history of heart research will help us to better understand the increasing attention given to the role of anger and hostility in cardiovascular disease. In 1900, deaths from strokes and heart attacks accounted for only 20 per cent of all US deaths. By the 1950s, shortly after the end of World War II, this figure had risen nearly threefold, to

55 per cent. While the US had become the world's hardworking miracle, its men were suffering a coronary epidemic. American males, often in the prime of their careers, were twice as likely to suffer heart failure as a Dane, a Swede, or a Norwegian, and five times as likely as a Japanese man.

The Framingham Study

In response to this epidemic, the US government launched the first great longitudinal study of the causes of heart attacks. In the small Massachusetts town of Framingham, medical teams performed very thorough physical examinations on a large number of persons, and recorded and stored the information they obtained on data cards. Over the past 30 years, these records have built up an incredibly useful set of statistics on the most common risk factors for people who later suffered heart attacks. The risk factors that best predicted heart disease were: (1) elevated blood pressure; (2) high levels of cholesterol; and (3) cigarette smoking.

The widely publicised findings on risk factors for heart disease identified in the Framingham study slowly led the medical profession and the public away from a widespread fatalism about the heart. Rather than blaming genetics and the body's automatic and involuntary workings, it now appeared possible to reduce the risk of heart attack if people stopped smoking, reduced their cholesterol, and lowered blood pressure by lifestyle changes or medication. The value of physical exercise also began to claim serious attention when President Dwight D. Eisenhower suffered a heart attack, and his cardiologist followed up on Russian experiments that used exercise to rehabilitate coronary survivors. An awareness of the benefits of exercise and nutrition in preventing heart attacks has gradually evolved. Although the facts are still being debated in scientific circles, millions of dieting, jogging people are convinced.

Type A Behaviour and Your Heart: The Western Collaborative Group Study

Over the past 20 years, new research findings suggest that feelings and emotions may be just as important as exercise and nutrition in the prevention of heart disease. Two San Francisco cardiologists, Myer Friedman, MD, and Ray H. Rosenman, MD, have conducted pioneering scientific studies of non-physical risk factors for coronary heart disease. The fact that a number of their patients who suffered heart attacks had never smoked and had normal blood pressure and cholesterol levels stimulated them to look for other risk factors. They observed that many of these patients, prior to their heart attack, were uncommonly ambitious, hard-driving and competitive, and always in a hurry. Such patients were labelled Type A personalities, and contrasted with relaxed patients, called Type B.

In 1960, after many laboratory studies of the Type A Behaviour Pattern, a second great prospective study of coronary heart disease was begun under Dr Rosenman's direction. In this study, known as the Western Collaborative Group Study (WCGS), more than 3000 healthy, middle-aged Californian men were given comprehensive physical examinations. They were also evaluated in a 20-minute structured interview designed to measure hard-driving, competitive behaviour, ambition, job involvement, and an obsessive urgency about time. On the basis of this interview each man was categorised as either Type A or Type B.

The facts soon confirmed the Type A theory. Over the next eight-and-a-half years, more than twice as many Type As suffered heart attacks as Type Bs, even when the other risk factors (high blood pressure, cholesterol level, smoking) were statistically controlled. Since then, numerous studies using different tests and interviews have verified the connection between Type A behaviour and heart disease. In most of these studies three major components of Type A behaviour have been identified:

1   a competitive, hard-driving lifestyle
2   a sense of time urgency that combines speed and impatience with an obsessive concern to do more and more in less and less time
3   excessive involvement in one's job

The Rosenman group theorised that the Type As were hard-driving and competitive, and maintained a rapid pace, in order to assert control and gain mastery over their environment. In 1977, probing even deeper, Karen Matthews, Rosenman and their associates re-analysed the taped interviews for a large sample of men who were between 39 and 49 years of age when they participated in the WCGS study. Breaking Type A behaviour into 44 characteristics, they used factor-analysis statistics to identify five dimensions of Type A behaviour. While competitive drive and impatience still seemed deadly, surprisingly, previous achievement, need for achievement beyond one's own job, and an emphasis on speedy activity did *not* appear to contribute to heart attacks.

Based on further review of the re-analysis of the WCGS interview tapes and WCGS results, Spielberger and London in 1985 noted that anger and hostility were the best predictors of heart disease, especially for men below the age of 45. The following specific characteristics seemed to be most strongly associated with heart disease:

1 potential for hostility
2 getting angry more than once a week
3 anger directed outward (towards others rather than at self)
4 irritability at having to wait in lines
5 competitiveness in games with peers
6 explosive voice modulation (such as the tendency to talk in loud, staccato bursts)
7 vigorous responses to interview questions (rather than calm, deliberate answers)

A single thread connects these seven deadly specifics; namely, hostility, anger, irritability, impatience, and explosive behaviour, which add up to plain and fancy versions of the hothead. These WCGS findings make it clear that the AHA! Syndrome is a major component of Type A behaviour, and that anger and hostility may well be the key elements that contribute to heart problems. Underlying anger was, of course, strongest in the Type As, but current research is also determining the extent to which anger is present in the Type Bs who suffer heart attacks.

Changing Type A Behaviour to Prevent Heart Attack

In their book, *Treating Type A Behaviour and Your Heart*, published in 1984, Friedman and Ulmer describe research on Type A men and women who had already suffered heart attacks. These patients were randomly split into two groups: one group was given traditional cardiological counselling; the second group received the same counselling, but was also given advice on how to alter their behaviour from Type A to Type B. At the end of three years, the results were clear. The group that received behavioural counselling had modified their Type A behaviour, and this resulted in a highly significant difference in the recurrence of heart attacks. The recurrence rate for the group receiving cardiac counselling only was 8.6 per cent, whereas the group receiving additional counselling directed toward changing their Type A behaviour had a recurrence rate of 1.8 per cent.

While Friedman and his associates have provided impressive evidence that Type A behaviour is a strong factor in recurrent heart attacks, their demonstration that Type A behaviour can be changed may be even more important. As was cogently noted by Friedman,

> No drug, food or exercise program ever devised, not even a coronary bypass surgical program, could match the protection against recurrent heart attacks that the Type A behavioral counselling program had been shown to bring about in a period of three years. (1984, p.14)

When a distinguished, medically trained heart specialist asserts that psychological counselling, designed to help heart patients change their angry, aggressive, time-urgent lifestyles to more relaxed, unhurried, and calm behaviours, is superior to any type of medical intervention, we should sit up and take notice. This is especially true when we consider the criteria used by Friedman and Ulmer in selecting the Type A patients for their study. They classified patients as Type A on the basis of exhibiting all or many of the following characteristics:

1. displaying facial tension and/or tense body posture
2. hurrying or interrupting the speech of others

3 speaking rapidly
4 tapping fingers
5 difficulty in sitting still and doing nothing
6 showing intense dislike of waiting in line
7 walking and eating rapidly
8 frequent use of swearwords
9 displaying facial hostility
10 being very competitive
11 having to win at all costs
12 trying to dominate
13 becoming very irritable when others disagree
14 having fixed, often angry opinions on political, financial, and social matters, and being defensive about these opinions

What is evident here is a convincing demonstration that angry feelings, hostile attitudes, and competitive–aggressive behaviours play a critical role in the onset and recurrence of strokes and heart attacks. Equally striking is the clear evidence that we have the power to prevent the recurrence of these coronary events by altering the aggressive behaviours of Type A patients towards those of the more relaxed Type B who have a substantially lower incidence of coronary disease. The effects of anger and hostility on elevated blood pressure, arguably the most potent risk factor for heart attacks, will now be considered.

Elevated Blood Pressure and Hypertension: Injustice Makes the Blood Boil
Early psychoanalytic studies of persons with high blood pressure revealed a link between suppressed anger and chronic high blood pressure (BP). If BP remains consistently elevated over a number of years and comes to the attention of a physician, this condition is usually diagnosed as hypertension. People also tend to agree that suppressed anger can cause blood pressure to rise. That's the origin of 'let it all hang out'. Psychoanalysts call this concept catharsis, and scientific efforts to verify its benefits have been ongoing for more than 50 years.

Let's now consider the findings of experimental studies of anger/hostility, elevated blood pressure and hypertension in greater detail. In a 1954 laboratory study, psychiatrist Daniel Funkenstein provoked anger in Harvard undergraduates, and then observed and interviewed them to determine whether they were inclined to keep the anger to themselves or reveal it to others. Funkenstein found that 80 per cent of the students reported anger as their major reaction to the experimental provocation and 20 per cent experienced anxiety. Of those who felt angry, about half aimed their anger at the experimenter, while the other half held their irritation or annoyance in and blamed themselves. Interestingly, the pulse rate of those who suppressed their anger increased three times more than the group that vented their anger.

In the 1970s, psychologist Ernest Harburg and his associates at the University of Michigan investigated the relationship between blood pressure and emotional reactions to anger-provoking situations, such as being verbally abused by a police officer. Individuals who said they would not become angry, or who would 'get annoyed or mad but keep it in', were classified as 'anger in'. Those who said they'd 'get mad and show it' were labelled as 'anger out'. Elevated blood pressure was associated with anger in; those who suppressed their anger also had a greater incidence of hypertension than those who expressed it.

The development of Spielberger's scales has enabled researchers to assess anger-in and anger-out more precisely. It is also now possible to investigate a number of commonly held beliefs regarding anger expression and elevated BP, such as:

- Hotheaded people are bound to develop chronic high blood pressure.
- Holding in angry feelings spells trouble, so let it all out.
- Only hard-driving, competitive executives and old people develop hypertension.

To learn whether or not hypertensives are angry by nature, Spielberger's T-Anger Scale was used to measure differences in two aspects of anger proneness as a personality trait. The T-

Anger Temperament (T-Anger/T) sub scale assesses how often someone gets angry with little or no provocation. The T-Anger Reaction (T-Anger/R) sub scale measures the frequency and intensity of angry feelings in responding to unfair and unjust treatment. In general, the two components of trait anger go hand-in-hand, but hypertensives are different. They are no more angry than people with normal BP when they are not provoked, but hypertensives get twice as mad when they are treated unfairly. In fact, they become furious, and remain that way longer than non-hypertensives because they suppress their anger.

Buried Anger Precedes Hypertension
While other investigators have assumed that people consistently either suppressed their anger or let it all out, Spielberger's studies indicated otherwise. According to this research, the same person let all the anger out in one situation ('When angry at my brother, I lose my temper and say nasty things'), but kept a tight lid on it in another ('When angry at my employer, I boil inside but don't show it'). Or she/he may react both ways in the same situation, getting openly mad while continuing to harbour intense angry feelings.

In a 1984 study of 1114 high school students, Johnson found that those who tended to keep their anger to themselves had higher systolic and diastolic BP than students who expressed it outwardly. Males and females with the highest anger-in scores had the highest BP, whereas those who had high anger-out scores registered only slightly lower blood pressure readings. But students who had high scores in both anger-in and anger-out had elevated blood pressure. Such findings clearly indicate that suppressing anger has a negative effect. Moreover, expressing angry feelings doesn't help if you continue to boil inside.

In summary, these results provide strong evidence of a connection between suppressed anger and elevated blood pressure. The research findings also suggest that repeated, inappropriate reactions involving the suppression of intense anger may eventually contribute to the development of hypertension. The findings of recent studies also indicate that:

- The same person may be prone both to express and to suppress anger, rather than only one or the other.
- Suppressing anger may result in elevated blood pressure even in healthy high school pupils.
- Unjust treatment more often triggers intense anger in those suffering from hypertension than in persons with normal BP.

Anger and Job Stress

Most people believe that stress comes in big packages — a major illness, a death in the family, or the loss of a job. They tend to ignore the little insults of everyday life. However, research has begun to show that, as these little problems add up, they take a much greater toll on a person's health and well-being than the rare major crisis. For example, imagine that you wake up unusually well rested, but then realise you forgot to set the alarm. When you finally get to work the boss chews you out for being late and then tells you your secretary has the flu! This means that you must, yourself, answer phone calls from angry customers, the Credit Bureau, the department store you have a dispute with, wrong numbers, and your cousin's girlfriend who wants to borrow your car. Between phone calls, you manage to complete some paperwork, although you could have accomplished much more if you hadn't spilled coffee on the desk. A typical day, so why are you exhausted?

Obviously, people have many different ways of dealing with stress. Consequently, recent research has focused on understanding why some people are more susceptible to stress than others. In order to avoid the double-whammy that results from a stress-prone individual entering an especially difficult job, it will be helpful to learn something about your own reactions to stress in the workplace. Therefore, if you are currently employed or, if not, can imagine yourself in a job you would like to have, turn to Appendix 2 and complete the Job-Stress Survey (JSS). Note that your Job Stress score is used in conjunction with your Trait-Anger score from Appendix 1. After you complete the JSS, we will consider the many hassles that contribute to occupational stress.

Our stress management clinics have included key executives of major companies who have done very well in their jobs, but who had become quite distraught when promoted up the next rung of the ladder. According to them, it was often the petty details of the new position, for example excessive paperwork, rather than the burden of added responsibility, that were the chief causes of their troubles. Although we were originally somewhat sceptical of this obvious conclusion, job stress analyses across a variety of professions has supported these observations.

Like most psychological researchers, we were deeply impressed by the pioneering work of psychiatrists Thomas Homes and Richard Rahe. Using clinical interviews, medical histories, and studies of more than 5000 patients, they identified 43 events or lifestyle changes that were associated with the onset of disease. These ranged in severity from major life crises (e.g. divorce or the death of a spouse) to relatively minor annoyances such as a traffic ticket. Because the Holmes–Rahe scale emphasised personal crises, few researchers noticed how routine problems such as changing work hours can contribute substantially to stress-related disorders.

Spielberger's research on sources of stress in police work gave us some early hints about the little hassles that build big stress. In a survey of more than 200 Florida police officers, Spielberger and his co-workers found that the 'Starsky and Hutch' type of drama does not produce the most stress. Indeed, when both the perceived severity of a stressful event and its frequency of occurrence were taken into account, 'excessive paperwork' ranked third highest among 60 sources of job stress and was rated almost as traumatic as physical attack. This work with law enforcement personnel provided the foundation for developing the Job-Stress Survey, which is based on research data from policemen, teachers, business executives, university and corporate employees, and military personnel.

Now, let's look at your scores on the JSS Job-Stress Survey. A score higher than 20 in Trait Anger (sometimes called the Temper Test), and higher than 9 in the Job-Stress Survey, is a potentially dangerous combination. Consequently, you need to make some major changes in your anger and aggression levels, or the way you handle your job, or both. It's a double-barrelled effect: If you have an anger-prone personality, you need to be especially careful in jobs that are high in petty aggravations.

Handling Anger Constructively: Personal Power and Relationships

How one deals with anger may endanger mental and physical health in other ways. In addition to the relation between suppressed anger and hypertension, and between Type A behaviour and heart attacks, researchers have identified anger and hostility as strong factors that influence heavy smokers to light up. Research findings also indicate that, so far as blood pressure is concerned, it is preferable to express your anger rather than keep it in, but doing so may lead to problems in one's relationships with others. We will now consider the role of these findings as related to our previous analysis of power, in which we noted that the manner in which anger is expressed is a critical factor in personal relationships.

Clinical evidence and common sense suggest that expressing anger aggressively by going purple in the face, shaking fists, saying nasty things, and refusing to listen is a recipe for disaster. While this may momentarily help your blood pressure, it will surely alienate other people, leading to a breakdown in communication and to additional undesirable outcomes. It is too high a price to pay, especially when there are more effective ways of expressing yourself and getting your message across. A better choice is to use the calm, assertive ways described later where we learn to deal with events that we consider to be unfair and unjust, and to deal reasonably and constructively with criticism.

Clinical psychologists, psychiatrists, doctors, nurses, social workers, teachers, lawyers, and the police are among those who must deal with the catastrophic effects of anger, aggression, and violence on a daily basis. Anger and aggressive behaviour play a major role in divorce, rates of which are soaring. Domestic violence is out of hand. Most of this physical and mental violence stems from the rampant abuse of personal power. One of the most disturbing features of all this is the fact that it is those closest to us who frequently bear the brunt of our anger and aggressive behaviour. It is well known in legal circles that the Family Courts and not the Criminal Courts are the most dangerous places to work.

How does this happen, and how is it displayed in the partnerships that people enter with such high hopes and expectations for a happy and rewarding future together? Part of the answer appears to lie in the fact that one or both partners bring hostility into the relationship, often due to lack of self-worth, low self-esteem, and feelings of insecurity. Moreover, the belief that one owns one's partner is particularly dangerous since it can lead to the arousal of intense jealousy and suspicion, and consequent monitoring of the activities of the other person. Jealousy can, indeed, destroy the people involved! Shakespeare certainly understood the destructive nature of 'owning' that leads to jealousy, which he clearly portrayed in the tragedy of Othello, where the main players end up dead despite the love they had for one another.

Relationships don't thrive when one partner constantly puts the other one down, with an unending stream of criticism or sarcasm. While no one wants to be the recipient of sarcastic remarks, unfortunately it is in close relationships that sarcasm most often flourishes. Belittling others is a strong indication of the use of power to defend against one's own sense of inferiority.

Ignoring or shutting a partner out of your life is another road to disaster. Yet angry and aggressive Type A people often do just that. Consider the case of a business executive who normally works fourteen hours a day, six days a week. He leaves home before his wife is awake and returns late in the evening. After a few drinks, he eats while reading the paper and then goes to bed. On weekends he claims that he needs to relax, takes his yacht out, and returns late on Sunday having completed work-related activities using his laptop computer on the boat. On returning home one night, he is greatly astonished to find that his estranged wife and children have packed up and left.

Vengeance towards a partner is equally disastrous. It makes no difference whether the punishment takes the form of ignoring the other, shoving, pushing or punching, refusing to speak for long periods, or withholding sex, praise or information. Punishment doesn't solve the real problem. It simply alienates the other person. Generally speaking, anyone who abuses his or her power in a close relationship is setting up the collapse of that relationship. Even if such actions do not result in separation or divorce, the rewarding and fulfilling relationship which is so essential for our happiness and contentment cannot exist.

Angry, aggressive people operate on fear. Instilling fear in others through menacing facial expressions, threats or attacks is an attempt to manipulate, control and dominate, and thus usurp others' power. This selfish, self-centred behaviour clearly doesn't work. According to an ancient Chinese proverb, 'The fire you kindle for your enemy often burns you more than him'. The more we study anger, the more conscious of its irony we become. Is justice really blind as she holds up her scales, or does she peer out from under the blindfold to render pain to those who trade in rage and fury? If so, we have good reasons to control the most self-centred of all emotions — old-fashioned anger.

chapter 4
Lowering Our Level of Abuse of Power

Anger is a normal, everyday emotion, one we all experience. There is nothing inherently wrong with feeling angry. But serious social and interpersonal problems can arise when we express angry feelings aggressively, which often results in poor or broken relationships. If we suppress our anger and boil inside, it can contribute to severe health problems, such as elevated blood pressure and hypertension.

Our anger level varies with changes in our environment. The same person may be laid-back and calm one minute, but furious or sarcastic the next, depending on what's happening around them. This brings us to the erroneous beliefs that some people have regarding anger. Many say, 'I can't do anything about being angry. My grandfather was angry, my mother was angry, my brother and sister are angry, and so am I!' The implication is that anger is an inherited predisposition.

Darwin observed that fear and rage were an inherent part of human and animal nature because these emotions were adaptive from an evolutionary perspective. Thus, everyone is born with the capacity to get angry, and it is certainly true that some people have a lower boiling point than others. However, it is not true that we are born with a tendency to become angry whenever we are criticised or get something wrong, or because we have to go to work every day on a boring job. Such angry reactions are learned habits, and anything one learns can be unlearned by replacing it with another response.

It follows that we should work on changing our reactions to situations that lead to surges of anger. This will require reprogramming our mind and modifying our ideas, values, and habits. Because it is so easy to slip back into old ways, learning to change the habits of a lifetime will require hard work and constant vigilance.

How to Lower Your Anger Level

Obviously, the first thing you need to do to change your anger level is to recognise, and then abandon, non-productive attitudes and beliefs, and replace them with the new attitudes, ideas, and behaviours that are discussed in this chapter. Unless you develop a new outlook, it will be virtually impossible to lower and control your anger or to express it in appropriate, assertive behaviour.

Learn to Recognise a Surge of Anger as a Warning

The warning of anger is: 'Something's wrong here. I need to calm down, consider my options for handling this situation, and then take appropriate action'. Your goal is to reduce the amount of time you harbour angry feelings once the surge starts. Many people allow their rage to last for hours, days, and even years. The longer it continues, the more harm it does, and the more difficult it becomes to fix the original problem.

It is essential to realise that, while feeling angry is normal, we should use these feelings as helpful signals to do something different about the circumstances that make us angry. Otherwise, remaining angry will generally lead to aggressive behaviour with all of its damaging effects. When we are angry we often say and do stupid things. Moreover, since unresolved problems can lead to a resurgence of anger or anxiety, or both, it is essential that we calm down, evaluate, and try to resolve the problem. By taking the right action, one that is chosen calmly and sensibly, we are in control of our anger — it no longer controls us.

Change Your Ideas of What Life is About

Humans are social beings who choose to live together in families and in groups. These various social and community groupings will survive only if individuals co-operate for both the common good and the individual good. Although it often seems that our modern world has forgotten this co-operative factor, the growth of cities and of modern technology has not changed the fact that we are still interdependent. The survival of the individual and of society depends on recognising this interdependence — our reliance on, and trust in, one another. To maximise the likelihood of this happening, we need to adopt attitudes that help us to see the purpose of life: doing the best we can to make sensible decisions, then putting these decisions into action. Co-operation (rather than competition and combat) and recognising the rights of others are essential.

Stop Living in the Past

Much of our anger concerns past events — mistakes we have already made, or mistakes we think others may have made. We become angry because we have been criticised or feel that we are treated unfairly; because we are frustrated in not being able to do those things that are most important to us; or because we've failed to live up to our own expectations and standards. In addition, people who have a need to dominate others become angry when someone stands up to them. What can we do about these anger-provoking attitudes and beliefs?

1. When you make a mistake, accept and promptly admit it. Use your mistakes positively by treating them as opportunities to learn something new; thus you avoid repeating the mistake.
2. To handle criticism when it occurs, practise the methods outlined later in this book.
3. Don't set unrealistic goals for yourself or for others. Keep in mind that everyone has limits to their abilities, and that anger and despair commonly result from unmet expectations.

In any area of human endeavour, only one person in the entire world is the best and it's probably not you or me. In any given situation, a realistic and achievable goal is: 'I'll do the best I can'. This attitude can become a meaningful standard in nearly all areas of human endeavour. For example, we can say 'I'll do the best I can to be a good mother, lover, or provider'; 'I'll do the best I can at work'; 'I'll do the best I can when playing games'. By always trying to do your best, you can break the competitive and destructive spirit of constantly comparing yourself to others.

4 Don't establish mental or emotional one-way contracts. Unvoiced expectations that require actions or reactions on the part of another can cause you to become angry if that person fails to live up to your expectations.

5 Don't throw a person's past at them in a hostile, negative manner or attempt to gain the upper hand by dredging up past examples of someone's 'bad' behaviour.

The usual reaction of an individual who is criticised in a hostile manner is to retaliate with: 'Okay, but what about the time you...', or 'You should talk, you're always...' In the end, the discussion deteriorates into a fruitless and damaging argument full of mutual recriminations, with each person heaping blame on the other. In the meantime, the original problem remains unresolved. The best chance we have for improving the quality of our life is by focusing on the present, and concentrating on finding the best solution to the issue at hand. Dominating or belittling others in order to get your own way just doesn't work.

Realise You Have No Power or Right to Control Others

It is our trying to make others think as we think, act as we act, or agree with us in all matters that causes problems. For example, it seems as if most of today's adolescents believe that rock is the only worthwhile music, and that the only way to listen to it is at full volume, a level close to the pain threshold for many adults. Telling them to 'Turn that thing down!' seldom works, and even if it does, the result is only temporary. A more effective means of achieving quiet is by discussing your right to peace. A direct, frontal attack rarely works because it fails to recognise and respect the right of others to be different.

Sadly, in today's world the excesses of anger, aggression and violence are most evident within families. Nowhere is this more evident than in marriages and other intimate relationships. The struggle for dominance, often fuelled by basic feelings of insecurity as well as by emotional immaturity, leads to a battleground with two people pitted against one another in a constant state of warfare, punctuated by numerous cease-fires and fruitless attempts to negotiate peace settlements — all because the warring parties have failed to accept the realities of personal power.

Real power resides in our ability to communicate in a calm, relaxed manner, as we try to persuade others to see things our way. Of course, communicating like this won't always work and we must accept that as well. The other person may be looking at the issue from a different perspective, may have a different set of values or may be just pig-headed and stubborn. If we simply do the best we can, however, it really doesn't matter because even if we don't succeed we don't have to get angry!

Recognise the Serious Limitations to Running Your Own Life

To begin with, it is essential to recognise that perfection in most things is impossible! Don't try to be the 'perfect' parent, the 'perfect' partner, the 'perfect' employee or employer; just be the best that you can be. Secondly, acknowledge the fact that you have your own weaknesses. Anyone who refuses to recognise and acknowledge a weakness is living a lie. Finally, accept mistakes as inevitable. It is futile to get angry at frustrating objects or situations, or with ourselves or others when we make mistakes. Learn to admit that you have blown it, fix it if you can, and try not to repeat the error, but don't wallow in self-pity, guilt, or shame. Instead of feeling sorry for yourself, say 'What do I do now to run things in a better way? What action can I take to get myself out of this mess I've created?'

Change Your Focus from Yourself

This principle is illustrated by the diagram in Figure 4.1. The circle on the left places the self at the centre of the universe with all others on the outer edge. This is the arrogant, self-centred view adopted by an angry, aggressive person.

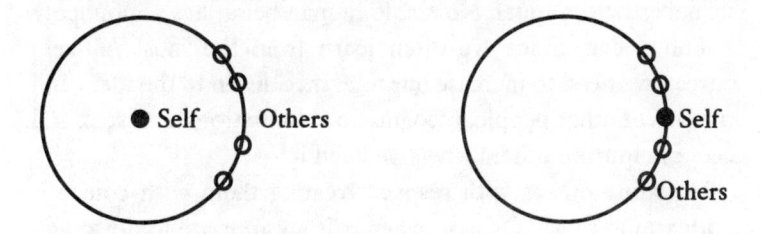

Figure 4.1 Self as centre of universe theory

Now look at the circle on the right. It represents the outlook adopted by calm, assertive people. Here the self is on the outside of the circle alongside other human beings. Calm, assertive people realise that everyone is unique and has special qualities. However, they regard themselves as normal, and accept the fact that they are not at the centre of the universe and that from time to time, like everyone else, they will make mistakes. Conversely, angry men and women have the curious belief that they should be able to get everything right, so they become perfectionists. For them, anything less than perfection is a catastrophe that is likely to result in criticism and ridicule.

Calm, mature, assertive people accept the world as it really is; they readily agree that they are not perfect and that sometimes they make mistakes. Their conversation is not filled with 'I', 'me', 'mine', and 'my'. Instead, they concentrate on the problem to be solved, or the choice that has to be made. Such an approach is typified by thoughts or comments like: 'Well, what's the most sensible thing to do here?' or, 'What can I say to sort this mess out?'

Consider the Rights and Feelings of Others

Angry men and women tend to be both inconsiderate and intolerant, and fail to respect the rights of others. Change!

Tolerance and consideration for the ideas and rights of others are essential.

Change from a Competitive to a Co-operative Style

To do our best in life we need help from others, and the only way to get this help is by interacting with them as equals — different, but nevertheless equal. No single human being has a monopoly on knowledge. Since we often learn from the most unlikely sources, we need to increase our tolerance, listen to the ideas and opinions of other people, recognise our limitations, and seek and accept help from others when we need it.

Regarding others with respect, treating them with courtesy, and learning to ask for help when it is appropriate to do so will bring us closer together, rather than our distancing ourselves and pushing others away through our anger and aggression. As a result we learn more, improve our decision-making abilities, and relate a whole lot better to other people.

Learn to Be Assertive

Assertive people do not consider winning or getting their own way above everything else. Their primary motive is to communicate, to learn, to make sensible decisions, and to act on these decisions. They try to be open, honest, and direct; they do not strive for perfection, but do the best they can under the circumstances. Assertive people live in the present; they are problem-focused and solution-centred rather than self-centred. They co-operate with other people for mutual benefit, but don't permit others to push them around, because that would not be sensible. While they protect their own rights and feelings, assertive people also respect the rights and feelings of others.

Alleviate Your Sense of Time Urgency

Since time urgency affects our entire life, it is important for you to examine and learn to slow down the tempo of your life. To avoid strokes and heart attacks, you may need to practise slowing down. There is truth in the tale of the tortoise and the hare, and in sayings such as 'Haste makes waste' and 'More haste, less

speed'. So, consider and practise the following ten rules that will help you to reduce time urgency:
1. Speak more slowly and express your thoughts more clearly.
2. Finish your sentences and don't assume that other people will always know what you mean.
3. Listen to others without interrupting or finishing their sentences. Take a real interest in what they have to say and adopt any sensible suggestions they might offer.
4. Praise others for their ideas and contributions.
5. Don't get upset if you can't finish all the tasks you have set for yourself; do expect and accept interruptions to your plans now and then.
6. Eat, walk and drive more slowly.
7. Don't become impatient in traffic delays or at red lights. Be patient while waiting in lines and queues.
8. Include recreation, social and cultural pursuits, and family activities in your schedule. We can make time if we wish.
9. Don't skip meals or eat on the run.
10. Stop trying to do two things at once.

Recognise Anger, Hostility and Type A Behaviour

Hostility results from a complex set of attitudes and beliefs, and is reflected in angry, aggressive behaviour in dealing with life's problems. Those who exhibit it are often successful businesspeople, or company executives who attribute their success to their hurried, striving, and combative ways of living. They are unwilling to change, deny that they behave like this, and find excuses to continue on their destructive path. In striving for dominance and control over others, such people constantly abuse their power, evoke angry reactions from others, and set themselves up for strokes and heart attacks. Since no one likes being on the receiving end of hostility, they alienate others and generally have poor relationships, which often end in divorce or separation.

In 1974 Friedman and Rosenman identified an 'action–emotion complex' that consists of ambitious, hard-driving, competitive behaviour, time urgency and 'free-floating hostility' that they refer to as the Type A Behaviour Pattern. Recognising that you may be a hostile Type A person is a necessary first step toward changing your behaviour and using your power constructively. The following eight points, developed by Friedman and Ulmer in 1984, list the telltale signs of the manifestation of hostility in Type A persons and they provide a good starting point for self-evaluation:

1. You become irritated or angry at relatively minor mistakes of family members, friends, acquaintances, or complete strangers, or find such mistakes hard to overlook.
2. You frequently find yourself critically examining a situation in order to find something that is wrong or might go wrong.
3. You find yourself scowling and unwilling or unable to laugh at things with your friends.
4. You frequently use obscenities in your speech.
5. You feel that other people cannot be trusted, or that everyone has a selfish angle or motive.
6. You frequently find yourself regarding other persons with contempt.
7. You often shift the subject of a conversation to condemn Parliament, the courts, errors of large corporations, officers of the federal government, or the younger generation.
8. It is difficult for you to compliment or congratulate other people with honest enthusiasm.

If two or more of these descriptive statements apply to you, it would seem that you possess quite a bit of 'free-floating hostility'.

Hostility, Injustice, and Unfairness

Type As (both men and women), as well as persons with hypertension, react with intense feelings of anger to perceived injustice, and to events they see as unfair. A large proportion of these angry reactions are in response to criticism of their behaviour by other persons, or to their own mistakes and blunders. Let us now look at some of the attitudes and beliefs that seem to underlie reactions of intense anger to injustice, unfairness, and criticism.

An attitude shared by many people is that 'The world should be fair and just'. Take for example a man who applies for a promotion for which he considers himself the strongest candidate. When someone else gets the position, he explodes with anger: 'It's not fair! I've worked my guts out and I'm better than that clown they appointed'. This reaction is often followed by excuses, and by blaming others for the failure to get the job, arguing that: 'I had no chance right from the start. Jones has been drinking with the managing director, and buttering up the others by inviting them out on his boat'.

What the unsuccessful applicant *really* means is that *the world should be fair to me!* The applicant is not concerned with whether or not the world is fair to anyone else; his viewpoint is totally self-centred. Although such persons want to believe they have the power and the right to make other people behave according to their wishes, no one should be controlled by the actions and reactions of others.

Let us examine the basic notion that the world should be fair and just. First of all, the world is neither fair nor unfair. Some things just happen. While it is certainly true that people can, and do, behave unfairly and unjustly from time to time, we just have to live with it. In applying for a job or promotion, the most we can do is to try to *persuade* a selection committee that we are the best applicant.

Inherent in all of this is the concept of a ONE-WAY CONTRACT. A contract is an agreement that generally involves two people, or groups of people, who agree to terms and conditions for such things as buying or selling a car, a house, or the offering and acceptance of employment. The terms of the contract are discussed, it is drawn up, and then both parties read and sign it. However, in a one-way contract, only a single party is aware of the existence of the agreement and its terms.

In the case of our unfortunate job applicant, his one-way contract would read: 'If I work my guts out, complete advanced management courses, and have the necessary experience, I should be promoted'. But the selection panel knows nothing about this one-way contract, and would therefore feel no obligation to fulfil it. Moreover, even though an applicant's virtues may be known and recognised, they may reject her because of her inability to work effectively with others, her fiery temper, or for one or more of a host of other reasons.

One-way contracts are very common. They include understandings such as 'If I invite you to dinner, I expect you to invite me back' or 'If I am nice to you, then you must be nice to me'. Although plausible, these assumptions are not enforceable because we lack the power to control the actions and behaviours of others. Unfortunately, hostile people refuse to accept these limitations in their personal power, and they become exceedingly angry when others fail to invite them to dinner or aren't nice to them, or when their job applications are rejected.

So, our desire for change must include modifying attitudes and beliefs, such as 'The world should be fair and just', to more positive and realistic approaches. For example, a job applicant might profitably think: 'I'll prepare myself as well as I can, put a lot of thought into the application, and give it my best shot during the interview. It will be great if I succeed, but it won't be the end of the world if I don't'. Avoid one-way contracts that say 'It's obvious that I'm the best candidate; therefore you *must* select me'.

The list of harmful beliefs that can produce hostile angry reactions to perceived personal injustice includes a number of potentially destructive and self-defeating attitudes, such as:

- Life is one big competition where it is essential to win, to succeed, and always to come out on top.
- Wimps get nowhere. To succeed, you must always be strong and aggressive.
- The world is a dangerous place. If I don't fight tooth and nail, others will take advantage of me and I'll never succeed.

These attitudes demonstrate the tendency for Type A, hostile people to see the world as black or white. Either you are aggressive and competitive, or you are a weak-kneed wimp. Failure to consider additional possibilities prevents highly ambitious, aggressive Type A people from realising that one can be strong and resourceful, and act in an assertive, forceful manner, without becoming hostile and aggressive. It also prevents them from recognising that relaxed and calm but forceful people can be very successful. Because they work well with others, they are often promoted over the heads of their hostile aggressive co-workers.

Hostility and Criticism

Ambitious, hard-driving men and women are themselves often highly critical of family members and fellow workers, but they have a strong tendency to react violently when they themselves are criticised. Being critical of others is based on hostile attitudes and beliefs: 'Other people are not very bright, their thinking processes are too slow, and they are ignorant and inept. They slow me down because I am very bright, know a lot, think quickly, and can get things done in a minimum of time.'

Such arrogance, combined with an attitude of 'Time is precious, so we must not waste even one second of it', leads to frustration and anger, which is commonly expressed by interrupting others to correct them, or by becoming impatient and finishing their sentences. The attempt to control the pace of life by taking over the speech of other persons is actually unspoken criticism. Interrupting or ending the sentences of another denigrates and belittles that person. Such behaviour is rightfully resented by those who live at a slower tempo, who choose their words carefully, and who, in fact, may actually be more knowledgeable and capable.

The underlying motive for a great deal of hostility is the implicit attitude: 'Life is one big competition; I have to win, come out on top, and be in control of my environment'. However, we are all imperfect beings, with no legitimate power to dominate and run the lives of others. Consequently, we inevitably encounter individuals who are brighter, more knowledgeable and more forceful than we are, and will fail when the other person refuses to be dominated.

The overly critical, dominating, hostile behaviour of Type A individuals often results in conflict with their partners, business associates, and even strangers. The simple act of driving a car frequently evokes a stream of abuse directed at other drivers who are seen as inept and stupid. At home, the criticism often takes the form of barbed sarcastic remarks designed to belittle a spouse, or angry aggressive comments directed at children for failing to be at the top of their class or the best at their sports. For the hostile Type A person, sport is an arena of combat and warfare; winning is all that matters and even foul play is acceptable if it contributes to winning. Another detrimental belief held by many Type A people is: 'Failure is the worst thing that can happen'. Therefore, when they feel they have failed they are likely to become depressed or seek solace in alcohol or drugs.

Clearly, it's important to identify and modify the attitudes and beliefs connected with Type A behaviour, hostility, and an overly critical general outlook. Consider the following example, which illustrates why one wife reached the end of her tether and sought marriage counselling. Speaking of her husband, she said 'He's always been a critical S.O.B., but this time he's gone too far. The other day I was taking my turn using the vacuum cleaner in our living area, which is a very big room. While I was vacuuming, he grabbed the machine from me and turned it off. He told me that the way I was doing it was inefficient, and that I should mentally divide the room into rectangles and then methodically move along the top set near the wall, down to the next set of rectangles, and so on. This method, he explained, would ensure that I didn't miss any part of the room, and would use less electricity. I coped with that by ignoring everything he said, although I was boiling inside.

'The very next day, he accosted me while I was shelling the peas for dinner. To do this simple task, he insisted that I should do as he does and treat it like a production line, putting the peas in a particular place, shelling them so that the waste fell into a plate rather than onto the bench top, and cutting down on the distances I moved. I could see the sense in what he said, but I am not a robot and I'm not one of his damned computers to be programmed. What I need from him is love and affection, not direction, but he's too busy controlling my every move to give me any of that'.

During counselling the husband became indignant and extremely angry, shouting that he only wanted to be helpful. In fact, however, he was overly dominating and aggressive in trying to control and manipulate his wife's every move, even in trivial and unimportant matters. Since her way of doing things worked for her, and she wasn't hurting anyone, it would have been better for him to adopt a more sensitive and constructive attitude such as: 'Before offering advice, I should ask myself whether the event is important, or too trivial to make an issue of it'.

Managing Criticism from Others

In addition to changing hostile attitudes that lead us to be highly critical of others, we also need to modify our widespread tendency to react with anger and aggression when we are criticised. Very few people handle criticism well and, in fact, most of us become angry and behave at least somewhat irrationally following criticism. The underlying attitudes that contribute to such behaviours include:

- Everyone should treat me fairly and justly, but no one should criticise me.
- When others criticise my behaviour, they are really attacking me as a person.

As a first step toward developing a healthy attitude towards criticism, it is essential to recognise that no one is perfect, and that everyone makes mistakes. Therefore, it is appropriate and often helpful to allow others to point out our mistakes and show us where we have gone wrong. Criticism directed towards correcting a mistake is — or should be — accepted as a normal part of everyday communication. Since this helps us to learn and change, constructive criticism of our behaviour is okay, and can be very useful.

When others go beyond a sincere effort to help us understand and correct a particular behaviour, this is unacceptable. For example, if we make a mistake in spelling a word and someone points this out, that's fine. However, if they go beyond helping us to correct the behaviour (in this case, the misspelled word) and attack us personally, for example by saying 'You're stupid', then we need to do something to protect ourselves, calmly and with minimal anger.

The best approach to handling criticism is, first, to consider the different forms that it takes. There are two basic types of criticism that have the capacity to make us angry, and each of these can be further divided into two subtypes. The first basic type is criticism that is fair and just, which can be subdivided into those situations in which a mistake can be fixed and those in which it is not possible to correct the error. The second basic type is unfair criticism, which may reflect an erroneous effort to be helpful, or the expression of undeserved hostility in the form of a personal attack.

The best way to handle criticism of any sort begins by calmly assessing whether it's fair or not. If the criticism is fair and the error can be fixed, then admit the error and fix it. For example, you might say 'Thank you for pointing that out. Yes, that was wrong, and I'll fix it right away'. When we make a mistake it is important to learn to accept fair criticism. No one gets angry and the problem is solved.

If the criticism is fair, but the damage can't be repaired, the best way to handle this situation is simply to admit the error and then to try not to make the same mistake again. You might say 'Yes, you are right. I did make a mess of that. I'll learn from this experience and try not to make the same mistake again'. Responding to fair criticism by getting angry, or feeling guilty and depressed, does not help to correct a mistake, nor to resolve any problems resulting from it.

Handling unfair criticism is more difficult, but if anger is allowed to surge, the outcome can be disastrous. As previously noted, there are two types of unfair criticism. The first is where the person making the criticism is wrong, but genuinely believes you have made a mistake. The second is nasty, vicious criticism aimed at blaming you when you haven't done anything wrong. In both cases you must be assertive, both in setting the record straight and in protecting yourself from the unfair criticism.

After carefully reviewing the situation, if you conclude that you haven't made the error for which you are being criticised, or that the other person either doesn't understand or has made a mistake, then be assertive in trying to convince the other person that he or she is wrong. You might say 'I understand what you are saying, but I've looked at it closely and there doesn't seem to me to be anything wrong'. Then proceed to try to convince the critic that he or she has made a mistake, or did not take all relevant issues into consideration.

The most difficult type of unfair criticism to deal with is nasty, deliberately vicious, unfair attacks that will, understandably, provoke angry feelings. Assertive behaviour is needed to redirect the criticism firmly, but calmly, back at the other person. In a work situation, for example, you might be criticised as follows: 'You idiot. That's shoddy work. You shouldn't have a job here at all'. Instead of flying into a rage, you could calmly say 'Okay. First of all, I'm not an idiot so don't call me that. Secondly, I've had a good look at this and I can't see anything wrong. Since this is the fourth time in the past week that you've criticised me unfairly, let's get an independent opinion from the boss'.

A third type of criticism that has nothing to do with fairness and justice occurs when taste and aesthetic judgement are involved. This type of criticism is often found in discussions of religion and in areas where truth is a matter of faith. A common example is in music where parents and children might have very different preferences. Here, the mother may be listening to classical music when her daughter asks her to turn off 'that garbage'. There is, of course, no way to prove that one form of music is better than another. Although it's really a matter of taste, such situations can provoke ugly scenes in many households when entrenched positions are defended and a violent argument flares. A more sensible way of handling the situation would be for the mother to say 'I respect your right to like pop music, but I prefer classical. Please respect my right to be different'.

If we persist in retaining our old attitudes and beliefs, it is difficult to handle criticism in a positive manner. Therefore, we must try to modify non-functional attitudes along the following lines:

1. I'm not perfect; I will make mistakes and that's okay.
2. Others have the right to criticise me when I make mistakes in my behaviour.
3. When others criticise me, they may simply be pointing out mistakes in my behaviour, and are not necessarily attacking me as a person.
4. Although not everyone will treat me fairly and justly, that's okay because I can cope with unfair criticism.
5. Even when someone attacks me personally, I can calmly work out ways to deal effectively with such personal abuse.

Aggression, Power and Problem-Solving

Before beginning this section, it will be helpful to review the forms of aggression listed in Table 2.1 (page 10) in order to increase your awareness of the extent of your own aggressive behaviour. Then, make a commitment to yourself to work on changing these behaviours. If you have been successful in eliminating or modifying the non-productive attitudes that underlie and fuel your anger and hostility, changing your aggressive ways should not be too difficult. However, attitudes specifically related to aggression need special attention.

The first of these concerns the acceptability of aggression as a way of coping with life's problems. Every day our television screens and newspapers are filled with accounts of individuals and groups who have resorted to murder, violence and mayhem to achieve their own ends. When we look at the world, most of us are horrified by the extent to which nations and ethnic groups use warfare as a means of settling ancient grudges and territorial claims. At this very moment, there are probably 100 or more of these major and minor conflicts in progress around the globe.

Although we are often confronted with poor role models, we can nevertheless change our own attitudes, especially the ones that say that aggressive behaviour is acceptable in solving disputes. Apart from situations where someone physically attacks us, such as punching, slapping, kicking, or trying to run over us with a car, it is not necessary to resort to aggressive behaviour. In fact, even when physically attacked, it is usually better to select a non-aggressive option such as running away or calling for help, since an important goal should always be to avoid getting hurt.

An aggressive reaction to physical danger is not really the problem. Despite the increase in crimes of violence, most of us go through our adult life without being physically attacked. This is even more true of calm, assertive people because they do not act in hostile, aggressive ways that invite retaliation. The real problem is that men and women behave aggressively because they feel insecure and don't realise that there are better ways of coping, and because it is a simple, primitive way of dealing with the world. Therefore, we need to adopt an attitude that says 'I will not behave aggressively towards others unless my life or the life of someone else is in danger, or if serious injury seems likely'.

A second common attitude that needs attention is related to strength and power. While there are whole sets of such attitudes, the main one is: 'Unless I respond aggressively, others will think I am a wimp — a weak-kneed person who is an easy mark'. Even if others think this, it really doesn't matter so long as we use our own power well. If we firmly and calmly prevent others from stripping us of our power, we are in charge and can resist the attacks of hostile people without ourselves resorting to aggression.

The paradox is clear. Aggressive behaviour is often a sign of weakness rather than strength. It is also a sign of inability to cope effectively with anger-provoking circumstances. On the other hand, those who remain calm, work out the most sensible solution to a problem, and then effectively achieve this solution, are the strong, powerful, and resourceful ones. And when it is difficult to determine a sensible way of dealing with a situation, the strong and powerful ask for help from others. In contrast, hostile aggressive people typically refuse to seek help because they see this as a sign of weakness when, in fact, it is really a sign of strength. Therefore, the most appropriate attitude might be:

'Asking for help when necessary is not a weakness, but a sign of strength and resourcefulness'. A resourceful person is strong and powerful. Being resourceful, clever, ingenious and inventive involves getting help from people with skills and knowledge that we don't possess.

In controlling the experience and expression of anger, it is important to be aware of our hostile attitudes and the particular areas in which our angry feelings are expressed in aggressive behaviour. Some people express hostility in many aspects of their lives. It may permeate everything, from exploding in trivial situations such as having no soap in the shower or being unable to find our car keys, to very serious situations such as business failure and bankruptcy where Type A men and women sometimes resort to the most aggressive act of all — self-destruction. Before concluding this chapter, let us consider three aspects of anger, hostility and aggression that often result in major problems:

1   self-righteous anger
2   transferring anger from one situation to another
3   the guilt that may be experienced when anger is expressed

Anger, Self-Righteousness and Guilt

With regard to *self-righteous anger*, aren't we well within our rights in holding on to our anger when others are responsible for it? Absolutely not! The principles regarding anger and aggression don't change, no matter who or what the cause. Holding on to anger is detrimental and not in our own best interests. Self-righteous or justifiable anger, as it is sometimes called, results when we maintain our rage because it is obvious to us that we have been harmed by someone else. It's all their fault. In fact, we may even exult in our anger because it gives us a feeling of superiority over other persons. However, it really does hurt us. For example, suppose a woman belongs to an organisation such as a tennis club or public-speaking group. Someone in the organisation says something that makes her angry and she leaves. On returning to her home, she is cross with her husband and snaps at her children, thus spreading her anger from the person who 'caused' the problem to others who are innocent. Her feelings are hurt, she has upset the family by her anger, and she may no longer derive benefit or pleasure from an activity she once enjoyed.

If it is allowed to simmer, self-righteous anger can lead to long estrangements between family members and friends. Therefore, we need to take responsibility for our own behaviour and divorce it from the original problem. While the person who caused us to feel angry may have been wrong in unfairly attacking us, we are responsible for holding on to our anger for days, months, or even years. As we learn positive ways of handling our anger, it might be appropriate to go back to the other person, apologise for maintaining our rage, and then try to sort out the original problem.

A second difficult area in dealing with anger is in transporting it from the circumstances that aroused it to another situation. Here we need to look at both short-term and long-term effects. An example of the former, where the effects were short-term but serious, involves Johnson, who put on his new, expensive coat, and found to his dismay that it was a bit shorter on one side than on the other. Johnson became very angry, but decided to wear the coat to a group therapy meeting anyway. During the meeting a group member asked him why he was being so aggressive. He replied by describing his feelings when he tried the coat on and then said 'I knew I was going to have a bad day, and I am having one'. On further questioning, it was clear that he had decided to have a bad day before he left home, and he had carried his anger into the group where it was allowed to interfere with his normally good relationship with other group members. Unfortunately, this is a common problem for many of us. We nurse our anger to the point where it poisons relations with innocent people.

The second example involves a young married woman in the same group who was behaving aggressively towards a male group member. Since he had not said or done anything to provoke her behaviour, he asked her what was wrong. Eventually it emerged that she had been the victim of incest when she was young, and that the group member was similar in height and build to the brother who had 'introduced her to sex'. She went on to recognise that she had experienced a similar response to other men of this build, but had been unaware of her behaviour until she gained insight into its origins in group therapy. Here then was a very pervasive problem where the anger, though certainly justified, had lasted more than 20 years and was still causing problems.

The third, and perhaps the most difficult, area related to the experience and expression of anger is concerned with feelings of *guilt*. Let's first look at situations where guilt is an appropriate emotion, and then at circumstances where it is totally inappropriate. The experience of guilt is appropriate if all of the following three conditions are met.

1. You are aware of and understand the effects of the action that hurts another.
2. There is deliberate intent to do harm.
3. You actually carry out the harmful action.

Let's imagine, for example, that you and another person applied for the same job and you've just learned that the other person was selected. You become very angry, and retaliate by running a key down the side of your competitor's new car. You *should* feel guilty about this action. After all, you weren't insane, you intended to hurt the other applicant, and you did so. Guilt, then, is brought about in this case by reacting with anger when someone else got the job you wanted and you, in turn, acted stupidly by damaging that person's car, and then turned the anger inward against yourself, which resulted in your guilt feelings.

In dealing with any form of anger, the idea is to fix the problem in the best possible manner. In this case, a sensible solution is to make amends for the harm done. So, calm down, admit your loss of control, and get the car fixed at your own expense. Risky? Maybe. Dangerous? Perhaps, but if handled the right way, probably not. By your admitting your mistake and making amends, others will understand and the guilt will abate. The one thing that *is* really dangerous is to continue to feel guilty, and do nothing about it. As is true of the consequences of any form of anger, if left to stew, the guilt will only get worse and could lead to adverse health consequences.

The principles are clear. When you experience intense anger and are fully aware of your feelings, plan to hurt someone, and then do so, you must make amends for the harm you have caused. If all three of the conditions that are appropriate to the experience of guilt are not present, simply refuse to feel guilty. Unfortunately most if not all of us do hurt others. But, if it is accidental and there is no intent, then there should be no lasting guilt.

In fact, much of the guilt we experience is unnecessary because it is based on situations where there was *no intent* to cause harm, and sometimes on situations where *harm was not even caused*. For example, the parents of a sixteen-year-old girl who became addicted to heroin blamed themselves for their daughter's problem and were racked with guilt for several years. Despite the fact that they had done their best to prepare their daughter for adulthood, their conversation was filled with statements like 'Where did we go wrong?' and 'If only we had forbidden her to go to that party where she was introduced to marijuana'.

These parents did not set out to hurt their daughter and they did not cause her any harm, so two of the three conditions for feeling guilty are not present. So there is no need for feelings of guilt.

Consider the twenty-year-old young man who persuaded his parents to allow him to use their new car to take his girlfriend to a party. True to his promise, he had only two drinks while at the party. On the way home, totally sober, he pulled up at red lights. Seconds later, a reckless driver piled into the rear of the car. Although the young couple was unhurt, considerable damage was done to the car. Months later he was still unnecessarily consumed with guilt. Did he intend to cause problems for his parents? No! Did he do anything to cause the accident? No! Yet, despite the fact that his parents completely accepted the facts of the situation and calmly set about getting the car fixed, this young man was so consumed with guilt that it began to affect his relationship with his girlfriend and he began to lose concentration on his university studies. Worst of all, his relationship with his parents began to change as he began going out of his way to do things to help them even when they did not need it. Remember, guilt is anger directed at the self and is very similar to depression. It is a highly dangerous emotion. Fortunately, we have the power to refuse to feel guilty whenever it is appropriate to refuse.

chapter 5
Managing Fear and Anxiety

Everyone experiences anxiety from time to time, feels afraid now and then, and gets nervous occasionally. These are all normal emotions which, at low-to-moderate levels of intensity, may even help us cope with our ever-changing environment.

Take fear, for example, which at low levels can be a very useful emotion. It keeps us from walking in front of cars and trucks, or standing too close to the edge of a cliff, and prevents us from putting our hands into boiling water or a blazing fire. Indeed, fear literally keeps us alive by helping us to avoid situations where there is a *real and present danger to our physical well-being*.

At very high levels, however, fear can seriously impair quality of life and severely restrict one's range of activities. For example, some people suffer such intense fear of heights that they can't even climb a small stepladder, let alone get on the roof to fix a broken tile. When they go on holidays, they miss some of the most wonderful scenery because it entails travelling to the top of a mountain in a cable car. Others have an overdeveloped fear of water, so they miss out on all the delights of swimming, boating, sailing, waterskiing, and so on. Such high levels of fear of specific objects or events are called phobias.

We certainly need a healthy level of fear about heights. We also know that water can be dangerous, as can spiders, aircraft and open spaces, as well as a wide range of events and circumstances in which some of us experience pathologically high levels of fear. Of course, there are many objective dangers in the world, but responding with excessively high levels of fear is not generally in our best interests. On the other hand, if someone is threatening to shoot you or push you off the edge of a cliff, experiencing fear might prove to be quite adaptive in motivating behaviours that help you to cope with the danger.

Similar to fear, which is an emotional response to a real physical danger, *anxiety is an emotional reaction to perceived threats to our psychological well-being*. As noted in Chapter 2, we may become anxious in situations where we are asking (or thinking of asking) for a rise or the loan of money, or simply inviting someone to dinner. We may also experience anxiety if we are asked to make a speech or to appear on television, even though there is no threat to our physical well-being. Rather, the threat is to our psychological welfare or self-esteem, because we are afraid we might perform poorly and be judged inadequate, or might fail and be rejected by someone whose opinions are important to us.

Like fear, low to moderate levels of anxiety can be advantageous if they stir us into activity. For example, a moderate level of anxiety might stimulate a student to devote adequate time to study before an examination, or to do research and develop a thoughtfully organised outline in preparing to give a speech. In contrast, very high levels of anxiety impair concentration, cause a person to move frantically from one area of study to another, and may even render us totally immobilised. At extremely high levels of anxiety, often labelled as panic, we may lose control and even collapse.

In summary, it is clear that the level of intensity of the fear and anxiety that we experience is critically important in understanding these emotions and how they affect our behaviour. Furthermore, as we noted in our analysis of state and trait anger, how often a person responds to situations with intense fear and anxiety is also important for personal well-being and mental health.

State and Trait Anxiety

Anxiety has two different and distinctive meanings. State anxiety (S-Anxiety) refers to an emotional state or condition that is experienced 'right now'; that is, at a specific moment in time. In contrast, Trait anxiety (T-Anxiety) refers to how often a person generally experiences anxiety as an emotional state. An individual who is high in T-Anxiety might be described as extremely nervous or 'high-strung'. The concepts of state and trait anxiety are defined in somewhat more technical terms by Spielberger (1972) as follows:

> State Anxiety (S-Anxiety) may be conceptualised as a transitory emotional state or condition of the human organism that varies in intensity and fluctuates over time. This condition is characterised by subjective, consciously perceived feelings of tension and apprehension, and activation of the autonomic nervous system . . . Trait anxiety (T-Anxiety) refers to relatively stable individual differences in anxiety proneness, that is, to differences in the disposition to perceive a wide range of stimulus situations as dangerous or threatening, and in the tendency to respond to such threats with S-Anxiety reactions. T-Anxiety also reflects individual differences in the frequency and the intensity with which anxiety states have been manifested in the past, and in the probability that such states will be experienced in the future. Persons high in T-Anxiety tend to perceive a larger number of situations as dangerous or threatening than persons who are low in T-Anxiety, and respond to threatening situations with S-Anxiety elevations of greater intensity. (1972, p.39)

In general, persons high in T-Anxiety perceive a wide range of situations as dangerous or threatening, to which they respond with surges of S-Anxiety. Consequently, they also experience intense elevations in S-Anxiety more frequently than low T-Anxiety individuals, especially in situations that involve interpersonal relationships that pose threats to self-esteem.

Let's look at an example. Suppose Tom has a very low level of T-Anxiety while Harry has a much higher level. This means that Harry is much more likely to report higher levels of

S-Anxiety in a wider variety of situations than Tom. For instance, Harry may become very anxious and agitated just before sitting an exam, when applying for a job, if asked to make a speech or when about to ask a woman to dinner. On the other hand, Tom may keep quite cool in the first three situations and only show a moderate level of anxiety when asking a woman to dinner.

High levels of underlying T-Anxiety frequently result in strong surges of S-Anxiety that can, in turn, have very damaging effects on the quality of our lives. Intense anxiety feelings can influence our health, educational achievements, and the way we perform in our jobs. Anxiety can also affect our social lives, relationships, and sexual performance, and even how we play. Let us now examine some of the research findings that highlight the role of anxiety in these areas.

Anxiety and Health

Perhaps the most important factor in experiencing a rush of anxiety is that we feel bad — really bad! The onset of an extremely high level of anxiety, or a panic attack, can be one of the worst experiences we have in life. Therefore, when we feel this way, the obvious immediate response is to seek relief from the unendurable distress. For some, it doesn't take long to discover the substances that can relieve this emotional pain. Although they come in many forms, their purpose is to alleviate anxiety and restore feelings of relative peace and tranquillity.

One of the fastest-acting of these 'anxiolytic' (anxiety-reducing) substances is alcohol and, of course, the stronger the drink, the quicker it works. However, the problem with alcohol is that the body soon builds up a tolerance to it, so that eventually more and more alcohol is needed to achieve the same calming effect. Thus, we may become so dependent on alcohol to help us feel good that we begin to drink heavily, and our whole life begins to disintegrate. Clinical studies indicate that a high percentage of alcoholic people continue their drinking careers in order to lower the high levels of anxiety they experience in their social lives. There is also compelling evidence to suggest that proneness to the use of alcohol to reduce anxiety may be inherited, and that alcoholism is a more widespread problem than is commonly believed. Some authorities cite rates as high as 10 per cent of the population as being at risk.

A second group of substances that relieve anxiety are prescribed tranquillisers, which have the advantage of being odourless, easily carried about in pockets and handbags, and readily swallowed without being observed. As with pain-killers and sleeping tablets, tranquillisers are highly addictive, resulting in similar or sometimes worse problems than alcohol addiction. Indeed, the withdrawal problems from anxiolytic drugs are generally far worse than from alcohol. For individuals who are trying to conquer their addiction to these drugs, it is quite common to experience distressing withdrawal symptoms for many months, whereas the most severe symptoms accompanying withdrawal from alcohol last only about a week.

In Australia, approximately 85 per cent of the prescriptions for legal tranquillisers, mainly the benzodiazepam group, are written for women. This does *not* mean that women are more anxious than men. However, it does suggest that females are more likely to report their anxiety symptoms to a doctor, and are thus more likely to become addicted to legal anxiolytic drugs than are men. In contrast, men more commonly use alcohol as a means of obtaining relief from their anxiety.

There are, of course, numerous readily available illegal drugs, which many people use to relieve anxiety. We are all too familiar with the reports of heroin and cocaine abuse, and the deaths that result from overdoses of these drugs. While it is certainly true that the use of illegal drugs poses a very real threat to individuals as well as to our communities, abuse of alcohol and tranquillisers, which is much more widespread, poses a much greater threat to our health than all of the illegal drugs combined, because of the volume of usage.

Another major problem with both alcohol and tranquillisers is that some people use these drugs to try to prevent a surge of anxiety from occurring in the first place. So, before going to a party they may have a couple of drinks or swallow several tranquillisers, or even combine the two, with disastrous results.

The drinker is slightly intoxicated before arriving at the party, where additional drinking leads to drunkenness quite quickly. But the consequences are far worse for the person using tranquillisers. Two tranquillisers plus two drinks may produce the same effect as six or eight drinks, and thus severely affect behaviour. Indeed, the combination of alcohol and tranquillisers can prove fatal.

Anxiety and Education

Many of us vividly remember facing important tests and examinations at school and university where our anxiety reached such a level that it affected our ability to recall information. According to folklore, persons who are 'nervous' or 'high-strung' are likely to 'go to pieces' in such circumstances. Research evidence on examination stress and test anxiety appears to strongly support this folk wisdom.

The most consistent research finding regarding anxiety and performance indicates that high anxiety is associated with poorer performance at both school and university levels, as reflected in negative correlations obtained in a number of studies between different measures of anxiety and a variety of tests of academic aptitude and achievement. The negative correlations between anxiety and achievement tend to increase at the higher secondary school levels, provided that the anxiety scales are given in reasonably close proximity to the achievement test. At tertiary level, anxiety also tends to be associated with lower academic performance and higher drop-out rates.

In addition to the evidence that anxiety has an adverse impact on educational achievement, other studies show a number of indirect effects of high anxiety on school performance. For example, highly anxious children are self-disparaging, shy, intellectually inhibited, have a strong tendency to daydream, and possess more negative personality characteristics than their less anxious peers. Classmates appear to react unfavourably towards them, while teachers, after the first few years, see such children as possessing characteristics that Western culture regards as negative and unfavourable.

Educational psychologists suggest that one of the primary roles of a skilful teacher, especially during the elementary school years, is to promote and sustain a positive self-concept in the child. This idea, as expressed in the work of developmental psychologists such as Havighurst and Erikson, emphasises the cumulative negative impact of a child's failure to achieve the tasks characteristic of the particular developmental stage. Thus, if high anxiety interferes with academic achievement, and teachers are not able to identify the high-anxious child and take steps to promote a more positive self-concept, this child will fail to achieve a positive sense of identity, which many psychologists consider necessary for successful personality development in later childhood and adolescence.

The way examinations are conducted can produce markedly different results for high-anxious students. In a study conducted in Australia by one of the authors, the performance of high- and low-anxious seventh and eighth year students from 14 different schools was compared using two different assessment methods. These were:

1 'Progressive assessment', which was based on short tests covering class assignments. These tests were given during regular class periods, often in an informal manner and without stringent time limits.
2 'Terminal assessment', which consisted of examinations conducted outside the classroom. These tests were generally given in the school auditorium, with strict time limits, and were followed by written reports to the parents.

The results were clear-cut. For both methods of assessment, the high-anxious children received lower grades than low-anxious children of comparable ability. However, the difference in scores was much more in favour of the low-anxious students in the more stressful, 'terminal' examination condition. These findings indicate that the higher the stress level during an examination, the greater is the negative effect on the performance of high-anxious children.

Anxiety in the Workplace

Anxiety often impairs the performance of talented individuals who should be at or near the top of their professions, but who are, in fact, much further down the promotion ladder. This may result from a fear of rejection, which prevents them from applying for jobs at higher levels where they would be required to make important decisions, and where the consequences of any mistakes might seriously damage other persons. Anxiety also operates in business and industrial settings to inhibit the presentation of creative ideas that might be highly valuable to the organisation. Fear of appearing foolish leads some people to remain silent, and prevents them from taking risks that could lead to advancement.

The history of one of our patients, Anthony, illustrates some of the points we have been making. Anthony was shepherded into the clinic by his wife. He was obviously annoyed and angry that she had made the appointment for him and that she had forced him to come. It emerged that Anthony was a highly trained design engineer who had joined a huge firm in the lower levels of management but who, ten years later, was still at this level. His history revealed that, despite his ability, he had never sought advancement, but was highly dissatisfied with many of the operations and practices carried out by the organisation.

In a joint interview with his wife, it emerged that Anthony was always planning more effective and efficient ways of streamlining work processes and had made detailed notes and drawings of all these schemes, but had never presented them to upper management because of his fear of ridicule, scorn and derision. His anxiety level was very high and he had repeatedly refused requests from his wife to apply for promotion. During the last five years, his record showed steadily increasing periods of sick leave. His wife also maintained that his alcohol consumption increased markedly every time he met with frustration in his job.

After a few counselling sessions where the ideas about personal power were explained to him, Anthony became quite enthusiastic and began to work very hard at ridding himself of his anxiety and at becoming more assertive. With the co-operation of his wife and of the one person in senior management who believed in him, Anthony prepared a short submission outlining three of his plans to improve productivity, and these were presented to the managing director.

Some weeks later, Anthony appeared before the senior management team and answered questions about the details of his proposals. He made such a favourable impression that they created a new position for him at a salary more than double the amount he had been getting. He is now supervising all the changes he proposed and is in charge of a scheme in which ideas from any staff member are considered and rewarded if they lead to improved work practices and a rise in productivity. Anthony is relaxed and happy, his marriage has improved, his alcohol consumption has dropped to acceptable levels and, of course, he and his wife are now in a better financial position. The firm has gained benefit and profit from his proposals, and some of his fellow-workers now have an outlet for their creativity.

Many employees use drugs and/or alcohol to reduce their anxiety at work. Unfortunately, these substances not only lower anxiety, but also have adverse effects on job performance, interfering with memory, the capacity to plan and organise, and to carry out job responsibilities efficiently. Excessive drug and alcohol use also results in industrial accidents.

A third area affected by anxiety in the workplace is absenteeism, excessive sick leave, and lower productivity associated with the health areas as previously outlined. The loss of productivity associated with alcohol abuse alone can run into many millions of dollars, especially in cases in which such abuse is the primary cause of industrial accidents.

Anxiety in Social Situations

Our theory of anxiety suggests that mixing with strangers in social situations, making a speech, or giving a public performance such as acting or singing, will be extremely stressful for high-anxious persons whose elevations in S-Anxiety could be expected to have a marked negative effect on their performance. We suggested earlier that attempts to cope with such situations by resorting to alcohol or tranquillisers are fraught with danger. Another method of coping that is often employed by a highly anxious person is to avoid social and performance situations altogether. However, this solution is usually unsuccessful because it results in cutting the individual off from other people and social isolation thereby ensues.

When faced with performing in public, the physical symptoms associated with anxiety can be quite distressing. For example, we may begin to shake and tremble, get 'butterflies' in the stomach, our heart rate rapidly escalates, and our mouth becomes very dry. When these symptoms begin to overwhelm us, our brain sends urgent messages to do something to escape from this very unpleasant predicament. As a result, our mind 'goes blank', and we may become incapable of recalling what we were going to say because crisis management has taken precedence.

When we have been through such highly unpleasant circumstances once or twice, it is no wonder that we feel compelled to avoid similar situations in the future. It also explains why anything that appears to help us cope with these threatening events, such as alcohol or drugs, becomes so attractive.

Anxiety and Relationships

It is somewhat surprising that highly anxious people manage to develop close relationships at all. Certainly, such individuals find it hard to make the initial approach in asking someone for a date or telling another person they are attractive. Fortunately, the growth of the feminist movement has helped many anxious men by stimulating and empowering women to take the initiative and make the first move.

After entering a relationship, highly anxious persons often irritate their partners with their procrastination, indecision, and tendency to place the responsibility for decision-making on their partners. When the partners realise they are being manipulated, they may demand that we play a full role in the day-to-day decisions. Even though highly anxious people may try to meet these demands, their endeavours are usually short-lived and they soon revert to their old ways. Eventually, the inability to accept responsibility, and the tendency to withdraw or to become immobilised, infuriates the partner who is then forced to take total control, thus marginalising the anxious individual's role in the relationship.

A more subtle, and often unrecognised, area of concern in relationships is the timidity of the highly anxious person who tends to prefer well-known and safe ways of doing things. This unwillingness to try anything remotely novel, different or unusual can have very profound effects for the partner because it often leads to a life perceived as boring and humdrum.

Anxiety and Sexual Performance

One's sex life can be profoundly affected by emotional states. To understand the seriousness of the effects of anxiety on sexual performance, let us examine the development of sexual impotence in a man with absolutely no medical basis for his inability to perform sexually. Consider Ben, who has been married for twenty years and has had an active and satisfying sexual relationship with his wife during that period. He is employed in middle management with a large manufacturing firm. Rumours have been circulating about a takeover by a multinational giant with subsequent 'downsizing' of redundant management staff. Ben, who has a large mortgage and children in high school with plans to attend university, becomes anxious and agitated because he is worried that he may be one to lose his job.

When Ben's wife makes sexual advances that evening, he wants to respond, but can't. He tries the following morning, but is again unsuccessful. At first he gets angry, then begins to think that he may never be able to have sex again. In reality, there is nothing physically wrong with him; it's anxiety about his job that is causing what should be a temporary problem. However, for Ben, his impotence seems to be a permanent condition. Whenever sex is a possibility, he becomes anxious about another failure and, of course, this is exactly what happens. Even when the job scare proves to be groundless, Ben continues to be impotent. In desperation, he consults a sex therapist who helps him to realise that anxiety was the primary cause of his sexual problems. Anxiety is powerful stuff!

We chose Ben's story to demonstrate how anxiety can work in the sexual area because the effects were so obvious. Many women also have difficulties in their sex lives. Some of these problems, such as frigidity, which are based primarily on anxiety, can be overcome by recognising and dealing with the anxiety. However, frigidity may also be based on anger reactions in women who have had devastating and traumatic early sexual experiences such as incest or rape. Fortunately, such problems can also be overcome with appropriate psychotherapeutic interventions.

Anxiety in Sports

The fact that sports psychologists are now routinely called on to help top performers in golf, tennis, swimming, and other athletic events provides strong testimony of the important role that emotional factors play in sports performance. Specific to anxiety, there appear to be two underlying mechanisms that contribute to poorer athletic performance. First, there are the well-known effects of anxiety on the muscles, which cause them to become tense. Optimum performance in sports such as tennis and golf depend on being relaxed rather than tense. The same is true in cricket and baseball, where errors can result from tightened arm, shoulder, and leg muscles.

The second major impact of anxiety on sports performance is through its effects on a person's expectations. Anxious people tend to live in the future, and are inclined to be pessimistic about how they will do in sports competition. Unfortunately, these negative expectations lead to self-fulfilling outcomes, i.e. the expectation of a poor result is likely to be confirmed by poor performance. On the other hand, people with low-to-moderate trait anxiety live more in the present, and tend to be more relaxed and laid-back. Thus, they can concentrate on producing the best swing they can, rather than contemplating that they will fail to hit the ball properly. On average, the performance of persons with low-to-moderate anxiety will be superior to that of their high-anxious counterparts whose potential may be just as good or even better.

Let's look at one example where counselling resulted in quite a dramatic improvement in performance in tenpin bowling. While not the highest improvement in the performance of people who asked for help because of incidents connected with their sporting lives, the most accurately measured was in Cheryl, a member of a tenpin bowling club. This woman arrived at the clinic after being threatened with expulsion from her club because of an angry outburst following her substandard performance, which cost her team a closely fought finals match.

Cheryl had taken up bowling a year previously and had improved rapidly. In the six months prior to this incident, her accurate record-keeping showed her averaging 154 per game. During the last two months she had sought professional coaching. Her angry outburst followed three successive games in the competition where she averaged 108 and which included the final game where she scored only 98.

In the initial interview, it emerged that Cheryl's major problem was anxiety rather than anger. She reported that she had been having trouble sleeping the night before a competition match, that she was trembling and shaking early in the game and was extremely worried about what her team-mates would think of her if she didn't play well — all symptoms of anxiety. As expected, her high anxiety level caused her leg, arm and shoulder muscles to become tense early in the game and her bowls were spraying all over the lane. This early failure caused further anxiety and frustration, making the later bowls even worse. No wonder her final score was so low.

While Cheryl learned about anger management, the main treatment was for anxiety, with special attention given to her breathing and relaxation training. In recent matches, Cheryl has been averaging 182, an improvement of over 20 per cent on her pre-coaching scores, and an improvement of nearly 70 per cent on the average of the three poor games that led to her seeking advice. Her new-found control of her anger has also met with approval from her team-mates.

It is not only bowlers whom we have helped. Our patients have included golfers, tennis players, an archer, a snooker player, basketballers (both male and female), as well as sprinters and middle-distance runners. All but one, who refused to believe that such treatment could help him, improved their performances markedly. There is no doubt that if we take the trouble to use our power constructively by learning to keep our cool before and during sporting contests, we can make substantial improvements in our performance in competitive sports and especially in those where fine skills are involved.

In summary, we have seen in this chapter that anxiety can and does have serious detrimental effects on just about every aspect of our lives. Can we do anything to change these negative consequences of high anxiety? The simple answer is *yes we certainly can*! We do have the power to do this. Anxiety is not some mystical, mysterious force beyond our control. We know what causes it, and if we are willing to work at it, we can lower our S-Anxiety to bearable and acceptable levels. Keep in mind, however, that it has taken a lifetime to build up the underlying attitudes that make us prone to experience anxiety. Consequently, it will take time to change habitual ways of responding to those around us.

If anxiety is undermining your existence, you cannot afford to continue the way you are. Therefore, it is essential to regard the task of reducing the detrimental effects of anxiety on your life as perhaps the most important that you have ever undertaken. We do have the power to change the underlying attitudes that have such a profound effect on whether we get highly anxious or whether we remain relatively calm. With hard work, we can make substantial progress and achieve noticeable changes within weeks. To assist you in reducing anxiety and being more productive, methods for tackling this task are presented in Chapter 6. There is just no reason to continue to give your power away to others in what is almost always a futile effort to please them.

chapter 6
Lowering Our Levels of Misuse of Power

Before you read any further, check your score levels on both state and trait anxiety. If either level resulted in a High or High-average level you probably need to take action to lower your anxiety. In fact, because the average level of anxiety in most Western countries is quite high, even an Average level may be a cause for concern.

If we want to be less anxious, less nervous and less fearful, we need to make fundamental changes in the way we cope with our decision-making and our daily activities. This won't be easy; after all, we've spent a lifetime establishing the attitudes and ways of thinking and behaving that prevent us from running our lives in a sensible way. It's our outlook on life that causes many of the difficulties that beset us; in particular, it is our attitudes towards the people around us that underlie our anxiety, our nervousness and our fear. Unless we change such attitudes, we will continue to experience these crippling sensations.

In Chapter 5 we learned that there is nothing mysterious about anxiety. It results from a high level of fear of failure or fear of being rejected by other people whom we judge to be important in our lives. It occurs when we set out to please others and where we see disapproval or displeasure from them as catastrophic.

The main attitudes we need to change, then, are in regard to the roles we assign to these highly significant people. We also need to look more closely at the concepts of failure and rejection, and develop different attitudes towards these experiences.

Anxious individuals spend enormous amounts of energy devising ways to avoid criticism. Three of the most common are: (1) becoming a perfectionist; (2) putting off decisions by procrastination or indecisiveness; and (3) manipulating others into making decisions for us. It is quite clear then that we must adopt new attitudes in regard to criticism and making mistakes, and take responsibility for our own lives.

Earlier we noted that Type A individuals tend to try to achieve more in less time. We labelled this 'time-urgency'. Attitude towards time is also a critical factor for anxious people who spend many of their waking moments concerned with the future, and worrying about the *possible* consequences of actions they *might* take. Their lives centre around 'what if?' to such an extent that there is insufficient time and energy to consider the options for dealing with current issues and problems, and for devising effective ways of coping with what's happening here and now. When we spend 80 per cent of our time and energy living in the future, we are operating in the present at an efficiency level of only 20 per cent or less. No wonder our lives become unbearable and chaotic!

By holding on to our old, debilitating attitudes we give our personal power to our partners, family members, friends, co-workers, employers and even our children. However, it is possible to regain our personal power, to begin to delight in life and to have enjoyable and rewarding relationships.

Regaining Power by Developing Positive Attitudes

Somehow or other, persons high in trait anxiety (T-Anxiety) acquire attitudes that centre on an overwhelming desire to be liked and loved by those around them. They are motivated by the fear of losing someone or something they have, or of failing to get someone or something they want. Usually this 'something' is the approval of others. Rather than making sensible decisions and acting sensibly, anxious people go out of their way not to displease family and friends, or to do the things they think will please them. Such attitudes need to be changed so that they can retain or regain their personal power.

Many of us harbour the attitude that life means pleasing others and making sure that we don't displease them. Anxious men and women are often terrified that their partners, children, parents, friends and acquaintances will abandon or reject them if they say no to a request, if they insist that the other is wrong or if they themselves make any kind of mistake. Let's consider a few examples of the chaos and confusion that result when this attitude is the guiding principle.

A very important factor in all human relationships is communication. When one of the parties is highly anxious about losing the relationship, communication begins to break down. Under these circumstances, it is very common for scenes such as the following between Jane and George to occur.

Jane: We've been invited to Harry's wedding. They want an answer by Wednesday.

George: They're your friends. Do you want to go?

Jane: Well, yes! I suppose so. But you're very busy. What do you think?

George: I'm happy to go if you want to.

Jane: But do you really want to go?

George: I just told you. Yes. But they're your friends, so you decide.

Jane: But you mightn't like the people there.

George: Sometimes I could shake you. Why won't you ever make a decision? OK, we're going.

The underlying problem is that Jane's anxiety level is so high that she isn't prepared to make the decision to attend the wedding for fear George might not enjoy himself. Since Jane is a people-pleaser, she believes that if this does happen, George will reject her for making the wrong decision. So Jane manipulates George into making the decision for her. She may think she can't lose, but unfortunately she has already lost because George is now annoyed with her and wants to shake her because of her indecision.

A similar problem might arise when George initiates the conversation about an invitation that he has received.

George: We've been invited to my boss's house for his wife's fiftieth birthday next Saturday. Would you like to go?

Jane doesn't like her husband's boss, detests his wife, and had a miserable time at a previous office party. Although she definitely doesn't want to go, she says:

Jane: Well, I've got so much work to do around the house.
George: I'll give you a hand with that.
Jane: Oh! All right then. We'll go.

Jane has just said 'yes' when she means 'no'. She said 'yes' because of her underlying fear of rejection by George. Her goal is to please him, but when she goes to the party it is almost guaranteed that she won't enjoy herself, that George will sense this, and that the evening will end in a quarrel.

Obviously, the sensible thing is to have enough faith in ourselves *and in others* so that the communication is not based on false or unspoken information. Dishonesty in relationships is much more likely to result in rejection than honest communication would.

Another common rejection scenario occurs when an anxious person wants to say something during a group discussion. Consider one such incident in which a neighbourhood resident decided to attend a public meeting to discuss a local council proposal to build a playground on the site of what had once been a dump. It so happened that she alone knew that drums which had held very dangerous chemicals had been dumped there, and she wanted to make this fact known.

When the meeting took place, there was almost unanimous support from the individuals and groups who had attended in favour of building the playground. After considerable discussion, the chairperson asked if there were any objections to the proposal. Silence! Our resident had decided to speak up, but as she rose to her feet, she had a conversation with herself. 'Well, they're probably not interested in my comments. It all happened years ago, anyway. They all seem so keen that I'd just make a fool of myself if I spoke up, so I'll just keep quiet.' Fear of ridicule and rejection at work!

In the first example, all Jane needed to do was decide whether or not she wanted to go to the wedding and convey this message clearly to George who, in fact, was happy to go. In the second example, Jane clearly didn't want to go to the boss's house. However, instead of saying so, she told a lie. When this didn't work, she found herself saying 'yes' when she really meant 'no', a common response of the anxious. This tendency to get ourselves into undesirable positions because we are untruthful is an almost inevitable consequence of high anxiety. In the third example, the resident at the public meeting doesn't actually tell a lie, but she does withhold crucial information that could seriously affect the health of the children using the playground.

Attitude Towards Pleasing Others

To help prevent the chaos reflected in these situations and retain or regain our power, we need to replace our old self-defeating attitudes about life with brand new ones. The first new attitude that we need to develop is to use our skills and abilities to do the best we can whether or not it pleases others.

New Attitude 1 Life is not about pleasing others or keeping the peace at any price. We must co-operate with others through open, honest, and direct communication, and use whatever skills and abilities we have to do the best we can to cope with the situations with which we are faced.

Many people resist changing to this new attitude because they see the old one as being 'helpful, kind, and considerate'. In fact, the old attitude is none of these because it often results in behaviour that is unhelpful, inconsiderate, and sometimes downright rude! What we are *really* doing is trying to make sure that we avoid being criticised. There is simply no way to justify lying or withholding information from other persons that would enable them to make more informed and sensible decisions.

Attitude Towards Failure

The second attitude that needs to be changed involves the concept of failure. Many of us think that if we make a mistake, say the wrong thing, or do something silly, the consequences will be terrible, and if we fail, it will be even worse. What we need to do, instead, is to recognise and acknowledge the fact that everyone — ourselves included — is limited, fallible and capable of making mistakes. It is absolutely impossible to go through life, or even a single day, without making at least one error or mistake.

While it is certainly desirable to make as few blunders as possible, the way to minimise foul-ups is not through perfectionism, because that's impossible. We must accept our own humanity and the fact that we are not perfect, God-like creatures, without fault. All human beings are limited, and the sooner we accept this the better off we will be. Therefore, we need to adopt two new attitudes regarding possible failures: one for ourselves, and one for others.

New Attitude 2 All human beings are imperfect so we all fail every now and then. I am human, so occasionally I'll get things wrong, make mistakes, and find myself unable to cope, and that's OK.

Even though this attitude applies to ourselves, those around us, including our parents, partners, friends, and employers, have the same limitations to their personal power. Therefore, we need to extend New Attitude 2 to them.

New Attitude 2A Everyone I know is imperfect; so I need to learn to be tolerant and stop demanding perfection from other people who are also limited and fallible.

Let's now consider another aspect of failure. When anxious people fail in some task, there is a tendency for them to over-react and come down heavily on themselves with strong negative feelings such as: 'Oh no! I've done it again. I've really made a mess of this job. It's terrible and I'm hopeless. I've failed again; I am a failure. Why can't I ever get things right?' When anger is directed inward against ourselves in this manner, we are apt to feel depressed. Thus, when we experience failure, our attitudes lead to anxiety, which causes additional mistakes. These mistakes are followed by self-directed anger, which results in depression.

There is a big jump in logic here. To equate 'I have failed' with 'I am a failure' is just plain crazy. While it's true that everyone fails from time to time, this does not mean that a person *is* a failure. Sadly, however, anxious people tend to think this way. This habit of putting ourselves down, and denigrating ourselves at every turn, is a product of poor self-image. But, given our new attitude towards mistakes, we can now say: 'Well, I got that wrong, but that's OK because I'm entitled to make mistakes. I'll look at where I went wrong and try it again'. So, New Attitude 2 is further extended to include how best to deal with failure.

New Attitude 2B When I fail, it does not mean that I am a failure; it just means that, in this instance, I haven't been successful.

Attitude Towards Rejection

The next area of attitude change to be considered deals with the concept of rejection. As with failure, we need to adopt a new attitude towards rejection. An example of the outlook we want to change is illustrated by the following.

We decide to throw a party and invite our friend Marilyn to come. She courteously thanks us for the invitation but states that she's unable to attend. For someone with high trait anxiety, the tendency is to feel let down. The anxious person assumes that Marilyn doesn't like her or him, and feels rejected. In reality, it's more likely that Marilyn declined because she had a previous engagement, a heavy work commitment, had been feeling ill, or for a number of other reasons. Why choose the worst possible scenario — that she really dislikes us? Instead, adopt a new attitude!

New Attitude 3 If someone says 'no' to our request, it means only that. It's your request that they rejected; they have not rejected you.

Attitude Towards Living in the Future

Earlier we noted that time-urgency and living in the past can be problems associated with anger, aggression and Type A behaviour. Since attitudes towards time are also a major problem for anxious men and women, let us next examine this area further because unless we change these attitudes, we have little hope of lowering our anxiety level. However, before launching into practical ways of lowering anxiety by changing these attitudes, we must make an important distinction between *planning* and *projection*.

Obviously, if someone is planning an overseas trip in three months, it would be advisable to book an airline reservation as well as room accommodation at our destination. This is *planning* and we are doing it *now*. It is living in the present. In contrast, *projection* moves us out of the present into the future and may cause problems.

An example of projection related to forthcoming overseas travel would be to begin to worry about the dreadful prospect of arriving at the airport late and missing the plane. We embellish this worry by running a little scenario through our mind where we see ourselves at home, in a frenzy because the taxi is late. We then imagine the cab racing to the airport only to see the plane take off just as we arrive. This is projection.

Another example of projection concerns the managing director of the Australian branch of a multinational company. She has just received a phone call asking her to meet the plane of the vice-president of the parent company who is arriving from New York the next morning. She immediately begins to project, envisioning the vice-president informing her that she is being replaced by someone from the head office. Such anticipatory behaviour is clearly not in our best interests, and can definitely cause a lot of heartache regarding events that hardly ever materialise. We need a new attitude.

New Attitude 4 Planning for the future is something we do in the present because it is necessary and, therefore, acceptable. Projecting negative mental inventions into the future is a dangerous practice and, therefore, unacceptable.

Anxious men and women tend to spend a lot of time and energy worrying about projected unpleasant events that might possibly occur sometime in the future. They also worry about failing and being rejected, and form unrealistic expectations regarding what they believe is likely to happen. Consequently, they draw up *one-way contracts* concerning the way they think other people should react to them.

An important aspect of the tendency to project into the future involves constructing 'mental inventions', where we actually 'see' pictures of future events in our minds. In an earlier chapter, we considered the example of a highly anxious man who had trouble asking an attractive woman to dance. As he approached her, he *imagined* that he could see her looking at him, sneering, and then rejecting his request. Although in reality he was still some distance from her, his mental invention stopped him in his tracks and prevented his making his request.

The worst time for mental scenarios to cause havoc seems to be the middle of the night when there is little or no stimulation for the brain. For example, a young man who is planning to ask his girlfriend to marry him is trying to fall asleep, when his mind begins to race. As his thoughts focus on the next evening, he sees his proposal being rejected. No sleep for him for the rest of the night as he tosses and turns!

The problem with anxious people is that they often treat projection scenarios as fact, even when they are really based on quite inadequate data. Although behaviour is generally guided by one's expectations, it is essential to stop trying to read other people's minds or forecast their reactions. Just work out the most sensible thing to do, do it, and see what happens. To be effective and successful with this approach, we need a new attitude concerning mental inventions and scenarios.

New Attitude 5 Creating negative mental pictures of future events, where we treat the imagined future as the present reality, is better avoided.

This brings us to one of the most important difficulties regarding expectations about ourselves or others, either of which can lead to anxiety. Many people argue that a lack of expectation may lower one's standards. While this may be true to some extent, assertive people have a single standard that is applicable in all situations. It is 'I'll do the best I can'. Since we can do no better than our best, this standard is of the highest order, but it doesn't forecast an outcome that will lead to feeling rejection or failure.

One of the difficulties with standards is that anxious people usually set them much too high, are unhappy with anything less than perfection, and thus set themselves up for failure. It is far better to keep cool, give it your best shot, and then wait to see what happens. Very high expectations do not serve any useful function and, in fact, may create new or additional problems. Therefore, we need to change our attitude to focus on doing the best we can, rather than setting unrealistic expectations that predispose us to failure.

New Attitude 6 When trying to solve a problem or deal with a difficult situation, do the best you can and wait to see what happens. Do not form unrealistically high expectations regarding the outcome.

If we choose simply to do the best we can in all areas without placing inappropriate expectations on ourselves, it would be rather arrogant to have undue expectations of others. Ceasing to place undue expectations on ourselves or others enables us to keep cool, which leads to lower anxiety and better performance because we can think more clearly when we're not upset. Once we accept the idea that our power to control the behaviour of others is quite limited, and that there are also limits on what we can do about our own behaviour, the danger of unrealistic expectations becomes clear.

New Attitude 7 Do not have unrealistic expectations about the behaviour of other people.

Another way of looking at expectations is to see them as 'one-way contracts'. Although most of us wouldn't dream of entering into a one-way contract when selling a house or buying a car, when it comes to human relationships one-way contracts are quite common. Many of us who invite others to our homes for a meal have an unwritten, one-way contract that reads: 'If I invite you to a meal at my house, I expect you to invite me to your house'.

The general form of this expectation is often used by anxious people-pleasers; it says 'If I'm nice to you, you must be nice to me'. Thus, without asking others to agree to the terms of the contract, we set conditions with respect to our expectations about their behaviour. However, since we have no power over the behaviour of others, and they don't even know there *is* a contract, we will often be disappointed by their failure to respond as anticipated.

The solution to this dilemma is clear-cut. Decide what is the sensible thing to do, and then do it, but don't put any strings or obligations on others to respond. If you want to invite someone to dinner, go ahead and ask. They may respond in kind or they may not. If they don't that's another matter and requires a separate decision about how to handle it. One-way contracts are by nature self-centred and selfish. What right do we have to put someone under contract without their knowledge, and then get upset when they fail to fulfil their part of the 'bargain'?

New Attitude 8 Avoid the use of one-way contracts.

One simple way to avoid the increased anxiety that often results from projecting into the future is to be very careful when using words that are future-oriented. These include conditional words such as *if*, *may*, or *might*, and imperatives such as *must*, *have to*, *should*, and *ought to*. Examples of these are as follows:

'I want to go to the office party but, *if* I do, my husband *might* get angry.'

'I *should* get this finished before Mum arrives.'

'I *have to* finish this homework before I go out.'

'I *must* paint that roof today.'

'You *ought to* be nice to me.'

In all such instances, the action has not yet occurred. Although the event is yet to come, we have moved straight into the future by using these words. For example, to say 'You ought to be nice to me' is an attempt to force someone to do what we want. Since we don't have the power to control the way others behave, we'll often be disappointed.

When we use imperatives such as 'have to', we put ourselves under unnecessary pressure to finish a task. The best way to deal with imperatives is to replace them with words like 'desirable', 'preferable', or 'I'd like you to ...' Thus, instead of putting pressure on ourselves by saying 'I must paint that roof today', it's better to say 'It would be very desirable to paint the roof today', which gives us the option of doing or not doing it. There are numerous valid reasons why we might be unable to complete the tasks we set. For example, it might begin to rain, preventing any painting at all. *Must* and *should* are to be avoided.

New Attitude 9 Be careful when using imperatives that automatically push one forward in time.

Anxiety and Perfectionism

Let us turn now to perfectionism, an attitude that is often used by anxious people to protect themselves from criticism. There are five steps we need to take in order to change this burdensome approach to real-life problems. First, we must accept the fact that we are human. All human beings make mistakes sometimes, and every now and then say and do the wrong thing. The second step is to recognise that it's OK for you to make mistakes. Third, we need to accept that it's OK for others to correct us when we make mistakes. Remember, positive criticism is constructive and helpful, and there are effective ways to handle it. The fourth step is to adopt the motto: 'I'll do the best I can'. If we are not satisfied with our best, we may need to seek help from someone more experienced or knowledgeable. Finally, stop trying to please others.

Divine beings may be perfect; human beings aren't and can't be. To have perfection as one's standard is sheer madness.

Consider, for example, a highly anxious man who got married and then built a home for his family. Although his wife was thrilled because the house was everything she wanted, her perfectionist husband wasn't satisfied. The bathroom didn't seem quite right, so he ripped it out and put another in. Over the next fifteen years he replaced the bathroom twelve times, but he's *still* not satisfied. Meanwhile, his wife is ready to leave him because of his compulsive need to construct perfect bathrooms.

New Attitude 10 Stop trying to be perfect. Just do the best you can.

Anxiety and Procrastination

Another important area to consider in regard to attitude change is the tendency for anxious people to put things off by being indecisive and procrastinating. As with perfectionism, the habit of putting things off is designed to avoid criticism. The unspoken reasoning is that if a person does or says nothing, they can avoid criticism from others. In the long run, this strategy simply doesn't work.

We all have the power to take action, to become more decisive, and to stop procrastinating. Of course, such actions do involve some risk; we might make a mistake, or say or do the wrong thing. The sensible thing, however, is to learn that taking these risks leads to better communication and improved relationships, which means that life becomes easier and more satisfying.

On the other hand, if one continues to be indecisive and to procrastinate at every turn, life will soon reach a crisis point. True happiness cannot be attained without some degree of risk-taking. There is a little card sold in bookstores that says: 'A butterfly is a caterpillar that took a chance'. Life is about taking reasonable risks, both physical and psychological.

New Attitude 11 Stop putting things off. Learn to take risks. Think the issue through, decide what to do, and then do it.

Anxiety and Self as the Centre of the Universe

In our quest to retain and/or regain personal power, we must look at our place in the world around us. In Chapter 4, we observed that angry, hostile, and aggressive people see themselves as all-important; and that they will go to great lengths to force others to agree with them, bend them to their will, and come out on top. They see the world as one vast, competitive arena. For them, life is about taking power away from others.

Oddly enough, anxious people have the same centre-of-the-universe problem, although manifestations of their self-centred approach to life are quite different. Their approach results from their tendency to live in the future, and from strong habits of going to great lengths to avoid saying or doing anything that might displease others. The end result is that anxious persons relinquish their power to those around them. The remedy for this tendency to live in the future is the same as for their angry and aggressive counterparts. The easiest way to understand this attitude is by referring to the diagram in Chapter 4 (page 47).

The circle on the left has the self at the centre of universe with other people on the rim. Seeing the self in this way is, essentially, the perspective of anxious, dependent people. The circle on the right is the attitude adopted by calm, assertive people. Here the self appears along the outer edge of the circle with other human beings.

Anxious people think everyone is talking about them, looking at them, and, of course, judging them in a very negative way. Anxious people also have the curious belief that they should get everything right. Thus, they become perfectionists because they believe that anything less than perfection is a catastrophe that will make them the object of criticism and ridicule. Anxious perfectionists see mistakes as indicative of being hopeless, stupid, or a fool; they have the foolish attitude that no one should criticise them.

In contrast, calm people regard themselves as normal, mistake-prone individuals, and are not overly concerned with what others think about them. Non-anxious, assertive people accept the world as it is. They do the best they can and, because they have learned to handle criticism, don't get upset when a mistake is made and pointed out. Chapter 7 will examine in greater detail the concept of self-esteem and its relation to power. For the moment, however, we will simply note that it is impossible to develop high self-esteem, or even to like yourself, while adopting a centre-of-the-universe theory of life. How can you like yourself when you are always failing?

Sensible, assertive people handle this by concentrating on the problem to be solved or the choice to be made, where such issues, problems, and choice are placed at their centre. Such an approach is typified by thoughts or comments like 'Well, what's the most sensible thing to do here' or 'What can I say to sort out this mess?' This is in marked contrast to the anxious, submissive person who says 'If I get this wrong, she won't like me' or 'I'd better not say anything here in case I say the wrong thing'. Whereas the anxious person focuses on the possible reactions of others, the calm person focuses on getting the issues solved and resolved. In essence, the anxious person thinks 'I', 'my', 'me', and 'mine', while the calm, assertive person who is outside the self, looks at 'he', 'she', 'it', 'they', and 'them.'

The paradox in all of this is that while anxious people, with their emphasis on pleasing others, see themselves as selfless, helpful human beings, they are actually arrogant and self-centred. They are also living a lie. For example, consider the case of the woman who says 'yes' to sex when she means 'no'. This is a lie. Or, take the corporate executive who is approached by her boss late Friday afternoon and invited to spend the weekend at the boss's holiday home at the seaside. She hates her boss, but to please her says 'Yes, I'd love to come'. This is a lie and living a lie is a recipe for disaster.

Since healthy relationships must be based on honesty and truthfulness in communicating with others, falsehoods and lies destroy relationships, even though anxious people believe they are trying to preserve them and maintain peace. But this doesn't work when the entire relationship is based on lies. The use of lies and falsehoods in relationships stems from efforts to ensure that everyone around us likes and approves of us. Sadly, a further paradox is that the more we try to please others, the more we lie and the less they like us. The way to fix all this is to stop seeing yourself as the centre of the universe.

New Attitude 12 Give up trying to be the centre of the universe. Change the focus of interest from yourself to the immediate situation, and to finding solutions to your problems.

The next section deals with whether we allow ourselves to be guided and directed by outside forces, or try to become self-reliant and internally directed. Given the importance of maintaining or gaining control over our lives, one's reaction to internal and external cues, which is sometimes called 'locus of control', is of central importance.

Anxiety and Locus of Control

Locus of control is closely related to the concept of dependency. People who allow — or actively seek out — others to make their decisions, or who lean on others emotionally and are externally directed, tend to be dependent and highly anxious. On the other hand, individuals who are self-reliant and internally directed are generally more independent and less likely to engage in people-pleasing behaviour. Such individuals are usually low in anxiety and use their power well.

During adolescence, children should learn to become emotionally independent of their parents. Although they *want* their parents' approval, love, and affection, those children who successfully mature and become independent learn to make decisions for themselves. They also learn to carry out sensible actions even when their parents may not approve of their decisions and actions. If both the growing adolescent and his or her parents feel secure in their relationship, neither feels threatened by differences of opinion. The adolescent no longer *needs* parental approval, nor do the parents *need* submission.

Problems in adjustment stem from the fact that few of us handle growing up as well as we might, and most of us cling to at least some of our dependency. When we reach adulthood and marry, it is then quite common to transfer this dependency from our parents to our spouse. Because society considers male dependency unacceptable, a man's dependency needs — which might be quite strong — must be kept hidden and this in turn can lead to anxiety.

Almost everyone likes approval, and most of us thrive on praise. However, we can — and do — continue to function whether or not we get approval. But people who are anxious and externally directed permit their lives to be shaped by the approval of others; they desperately need this approval. Conversely, assertive people are internally directed and recognise that reward comes from inside. When they succeed, they say to themselves 'Terrific. I got that right. Well done'. When they don't succeed they say 'Well, I gave it my best shot. It didn't work very well, but that's OK. Now let's see if I can find a better way to handle this'. Internally directed people do not allow themselves to fall apart, nor do they give power over themselves to others.

This does not mean that assertive people reject help from others. On the contrary, if the sensible thing to do is to seek assistance, then they ask for help. Thus, independence is achieved only when we are at ease with ourselves, and can readily seek outside assistance when it's needed and beneficial.

New Attitude 13 It is dangerous to allow oneself to be externally directed, approval-seeking and dependent on others for praise. Instead, become internally directed, self-reliant and independent, seeking reward and praise from internal sources.

Anxiety, Blame and Responsibility

One final aspect of anxiety-ridden behaviour that we must consider is how we handle blame and take responsibility for our own behaviour. In addition to castigating themselves for their own errors, anxious people tend to blame themselves for many of the things that other people do and that go wrong around them. This problem is really an extension of the anxious person's centre-of-the-universe theory of life. If someone is in a hurry to keep an appointment, and bumps into you, he is the one that should apologise, not you. If a file is lost at work, the anxious person automatically thinks that she or he is at fault.

In order to maximise personal power, one must accept responsibility for one's own behaviour, including mistakes. When we make a mistake, the sensible thing to do is admit it, come clean, and accept personal responsibility. For example, if you break a valuable vase, it's not sensible to hide the pieces and hope no one notices, nor is it sensible to blame someone else as an angry, aggressive person is prone to do. On the other hand, it's foolish to assume responsibility for the mistakes of others.

New Attitude 14 Learn to take responsibility for your own behaviour, including mistakes and errors. When you make a mistake, admit it openly and honestly. Don't blame others for mistakes or try to cover them up.

To summarise the main message of this chapter, the best and possibly only way of lowering anxiety is by radically altering the way we think, which will require changing a number of long-held attitudes. Almost everyone who experiences high levels of state anxiety finds this intense emotional condition extremely unpleasant. It is nevertheless difficult to convince some people that it is possible to change. Others become so dependent on drugs and alcohol as a method of controlling anxiety that they are unwilling to abandon these chemical 'crutches' even though they generally make one's problems worse. At best, drugs and alcohol provide only temporary relief.

Making lasting changes in one's attitudes and lifestyle to reduce anxiety is not easy, but requires hard work over long periods of time. New ways of thinking and behaving must be developed before such habits become stronger than the old debilitating ones. For those who persevere, however, the rewards are enormous! It may even seem little short of miraculous to be able to face, with relative ease and tranquillity, situations we previously considered frightening or unmanageable. It can be done and many have succeeded.

Being anxious and submissive — a people-pleaser intent on keeping the peace at any price — is a sure way to relinquish your power.

Earlier in the book we described the aggressive behaviour that arises from an angry and hostile attitude to life as Type A behaviour, which we have now linked to the abuse of power. Type B behaviour arises from a calm, assertive approach to life where we are concerned with finding solutions to our problems and putting these solutions into practice by the constructive use of our power.

It is tempting to describe the chaotic behaviour of anxious and submissive people as Type C, but unfortunately this category has already been used to describe yet another facet of angry, aggressive behaviour. We have therefore chosen to describe as Type X those who misuse their power by giving it away to others. These people are characterised by high levels of anxiety and submissive behaviour.

It is possible for Type X people to change the attitudes that underlie their heightened anxiety, and to regain the power to run their lives in a much more sensible and rewarding way. In addition to making the attitudinal changes outlined in this chapter, we must also build a more positive view of ourselves and a high level of self-esteem. Accomplishing this without giving away one's power is the subject of Chapter 7.

chapter 7
Power and Self-Esteem

So far, our search for ways of increasing our use of personal power has revealed a need to work on controlling our anger, aggression and hostility on the one hand, and our anxiety, fear and nervousness on the other. We have also seen that we need to make quite profound changes in the ways we relate to those around us, in our attitudes and in how we look at life.

There are, however, other allied aspects that play a significant role in the extent to which we will maximise the use of our power. One of these factors is our feeling of self-worth, our self-image, our sense of self-esteem. Our attitude towards our self plays a large part in determining whether we will use the enormous power we all have to run our lives in a sensible manner most of the time.

If we have low self-esteem and see ourselves as hopeless, powerless individuals, as unlikely to succeed and even unworthy of success, we are most unlikely to be able to harness our power and successfully conduct our lives.

On the other hand, if we see ourselves as worthy individuals, if we are confident and optimistic of success in whatever we are doing, and have adopted the attitudes outlined in the previous chapters, there is a good chance that we will succeed in most of our day-to-day tasks.

There are many different ways of looking at the concept of self-esteem. Clearly, we need to reject any approach or theory that is allied to the misuse or abuse of power, and to adopt a view that is consistent with our assumptions about power and powerlessness. Certainly we have to adopt a theory that embraces the notion that we do have the power to run our own lives in a sensible way but that allows us to be less than perfect and to make a mess of things occasionally without feeling any sense of being a failure. Our sense of self has to be strong enough to resist the temptation to give our power away to others in our vain attempts to please them. Instead we need to develop a sense of self that will enable us to use our power constructively by being firm and assertive.

The Concept of Self-Esteem

The concepts of self-esteem and adjustment have a great deal in common. Those who are high in self-esteem usually handle their day-to-day affairs with confidence and success. These people are also often described as well-adjusted. However, it is possible to be high in self-esteem and still behave in ways that lead to constant conflict with our friends, family and associates, or even with the law. Many would describe such people as poorly adjusted. For example, a person might typically behave very aggressively and see this as the appropriate reaction to a wide variety of situations. Despite the fact that this response alienates and upsets many with whom they come into contact, and perhaps leads to the loss of friends, job or even to divorce, they might deny their behaviour was the cause, attributing the losses to the stupid behaviour of others, and continue to think highly of their aggressive ways of coping with problem situations. That is, despite it being quite clear to others that these valued personality traits were non-adaptive and self-destructive, the individual might continue to see herself or himself in a good light.

It should be clear from this brief description that being high in self-esteem is not necessarily a guarantee of leading a successful life, but it is abundantly clear that those who are low in self-esteem almost always lead chaotic lives, lack the confidence to think through problems and, even if they do, rarely assert themselves and put their solutions into practice.

The focal point of this discussion is the importance of self-esteem. Our lives have to be organised in such a way that our self-image is not only highly positive but also adapted to the situation that surrounds us. The adaptive part is crucial, because high self-esteem alone is not sufficient. In order to understand the two elements, it is helpful to look at two entirely different ways of measuring self-esteem, the normative and the non-normative.

The Normative Approach to Measuring Self-Esteem

In most research studies and in common use, a normative approach is adopted. Most of these methods are based on the 'adjective checklist approach'. In this method, you are presented with a long list of adjectives, such as happy, anxious, energetic, depressed, adventurous, aggressive, quiet, hostile, assertive, timid, submissive, extroverted, introverted, strong, talkative and so on. You are asked to tick or check the ones that apply to you. Your self-esteem score can be calculated in two different ways. The first way is simply by counting the number of *positive* items that are ticked. The second method is arrived at by subtracting the number of *negative* items from the number of *positive* items that are checked.

The two sets of items in the above list of adjectives might be said to be the following:

Positive: happy, energetic, adventurous, thoughtful, kind, aggressive, strong, talkative, assertive, extroverted

Negative: anxious, depressed, quiet, nervous, angry, hostile, timid, submissive, introverted

There are many problems with this method of measuring adjustment. For example, while most people agree that some personality traits or attributes belong in the positive or negative list, there is doubt about the placement of others. If we take the extroverted–introverted dimension, this aspect can be highlighted. In personality research, introversion–extroversion is considered to be of central importance. However, it is not yet clear how this is related to success in coping with life. For example, in one research study it was shown that the relationship between educational performance and introversion–extroversion changes with the stage of education. At the primary school level, stable extroverts tend to do well. In the secondary school the situation changes, with introverted boys and extroverted girls being high in attainment. Further changes appear at the tertiary level, where introverts are the higher achievers.

The point being made is that there is no clear relationship between introversion–extroversion and academic attainment, or, for that matter, with anything else — such as occupation, marital or social success. It is equally plausible to assign 'extroverted' to either the negative or the positive list. And there are many other adjectives that are equally difficult to place. For example, there is no evidence that rating oneself as *quiet*, *retiring*, and *sensitive* indicates either positive or negative self-esteem or good or poor adjustment.

The method described so far is the simplest and least sophisticated use of the normative approach. Basically someone, usually a psychologist, decides which adjectives belong in the positive lists. This judgement is often given respectability by asking a lot of apparently well-adjusted people to list or check the adjectives they think describe a well-adjusted person. Only those adjectives that a large majority agrees are either clearly positive or clearly negative are used in the final checklist of items.

The normative approach can be further refined by arranging the adjectives in pairs such as dominant–submissive, sociable–unsociable, extroverted–introverted, happy–sad. Different patterns of scores can then be related to people who are successful in various occupations, and these profile-scores can be used to guide people into different vocational areas. Quite clearly, different personality skills and interests seem to be required for success in the selling occupations from those required in the investigative backroom research occupations, for example. However, two people selected with quite different profiles may be equally high in self-esteem and adjustment.

Problems arise when one set of attributes is deemed to denote high self-esteem or adjustment simply because this is what the majority agrees upon. At a given point in time, the norm for high self-esteem for males might include aggressive, extroverted, not over-sensitive, forceful and adventurous, where it is at least possible that someone non-aggressive, introverted, sensitive, persuasive and non-adventurous might be even higher in self-esteem and better adjusted to cope with the daily problems of life.

The difficulties of the normative approach become even clearer when we come to gender differences. In many societies, different roles and characteristics are said to be appropriate for males and females. Thus, the well-adjusted female may be expected to fill the roles of wife, mother, child-rearer, cook, housekeeper and provider of sex, and to be submissive, compliant, warm, affectionate and loving, whereas the male might be expected to fill the roles of breadwinner and protector and to be aggressive, dominant, strong and dependable. Males and females are often taught these normative roles from infancy.

Now, nothing is fixed or immutable about what society prescribes as being the norm. With the changing economic scene, with changes in values and expectations, and especially with the rise of groups challenging the previously accepted roles of women, quite marked shifts in norms occur. In some places, the role of women is shifting so that many of the so-called male characteristics appear desirable. These changes in perception of women's roles are welcomed and accepted by some, and resented and rejected by others.

Clearly the normative approach does not allow an acceptable way of measuring self-esteem or adjustment unless we define them as *agreement by the majority at any point in time*. Those who are out of step with the prevailing climate of opinion are similarly assessed as poorly adjusted and lacking in self-esteem because they behave in ways perceived as 'abnormal' by the majority.

However, some of these people in fact are so well-adjusted and high in self-esteem that they are capable of leading social change. Conversely, it is possible that those at the other end of the scale who are resisting changes may also be well-adjusted and high in self-esteem because they have the vision to see and resist changes that are detrimental to progress.

It is a brave or foolish individual who will state categorically that the possession of a certain set of characteristics or ways of behaving will necessarily constitute high self-esteem and good adjustment on the basis that 'this is what society says', yet this is the very foundation of the normative approach.

In terms of what has been said in the earlier chapters, and especially in those about anxiety and submissiveness, accepting a normative approach to self-esteem is an almost certain way of giving away our power. This conformist approach is the one usually adopted by dependent, high-anxious men and women who search for some authority figure or a position favoured by an authority figure. Here is a position that society at large approves of. It appears to be an easy way out and to obviate the need to think things out for ourselves. When we do accept the normative approach, we will probably find that we have committed ourselves to positions and attitudes that don't sit well with us, but because of our fear of disapproval and of rejection, we say nothing to upset the status quo.

Fortunately, the non-normative approach offers us a method of approaching self-esteem that enables us to get around the problem of conforming to and becoming dependent upon agreement with the majority viewpoint, and that allows us to use our personal power in a constructive manner.

The Non-Normative Approach to Measuring Self-Esteem

A distinguished American psychotherapist, Carl Rogers, has developed a way of looking at self-esteem and adjustment that is based not upon what society deems to be right and proper, but on the 'congruence' between how we see or think about ourselves at a given point in time (the Self), and what we would like to be (the Ideal Self). If there is a large disparity between what we are really like and what we would like to be, this constitutes a psychological disturbance; we will be poorly adjusted to life, low in self-esteem, and our capacity to use our personal power constructively will be diminished.

On the other hand, where the Self and the Ideal Self are similar or near-congruent, then our adjustment and self-esteem will be high, our ability to cope will be enhanced, and our capacity to use our personal power in a constructive manner is strengthened.

The overlap between the Self and the Ideal Self that defines self-esteem can be shown diagrammatically as in Figure 7.1 and Figure 7.2. High self-esteem occurs when there is a high degree of overlap or intersection between the Self and Ideal Self as in Figure 7.1.

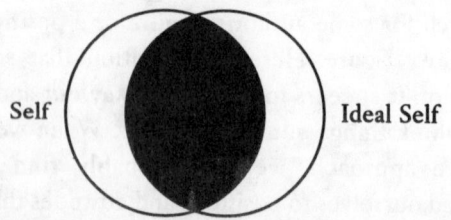

Figure 7.1 High self-esteem

Low self-esteem is found where there is little or no overlap or intersection, as shown in Figure 7.2.

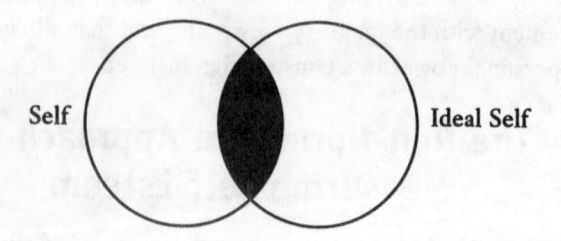

Figure 7.2 Low self-esteem

The process of building up our self-esteem is the movement of the Self toward the Ideal Self, resulting in an increase in the overlap between the two. Probably no human being is perfectly well-adjusted, so the overlap will never be total, but we can strive towards that end.

One of the consequences of looking at self-esteem in this non-normative way is that it is possible for two people with quite different and even opposite sets of characteristics and role preferences to be said to be equally adjusted and equally high in self-esteem. Consider two adult females who are quite different in terms of the way they see themselves, but who have quite different values and ambitions as set out below:

Self — Female A	Self — Female B
assertive	compliant
extroverted	introverted
outgoing	shy
dominant	submissive
leader	follower
career woman	housewife

Let us then imagine that the Ideal Selves of both women match and are congruent with the way they actually are. That is, Female A wants to be assertive, extroverted etc., and active in a career, while Female B wants to be compliant, introverted etc., and busily engaged as a housewife. Because there is a congruence between the Self and the Ideal Self for both, they appear to be perfectly adjusted, whereas according to the normative approach, one of them would be classified as poorly adjusted.

Under the non-normative method of measuring adjustment, conformity to social norms is not a prerequisite for high self-esteem, and this fits like a glove with our discussions about using our personal power constructively without being overly concerned about what others will think.

One factor that we do have to beware of when using the non-normative approach is our tendency to resist change and to retain attributes in our Ideal Self that are far from adaptive and that may even be extremely dangerous to our welfare. Take, for example, a man who is aggressive in his work and in his marriage. Because he has made a lot of money in the factory he owns, he attributes this to his aggressive approach. Consequently, he becomes unwilling to accept that it is his aggressive behaviour that is leading to the breakdown of his marriage and blames his wife's methods of bringing up the children for the problems in their marriage.

In terms of the Self and Ideal Self, he sees himself as aggressive, but as he can see nothing wrong with that he wants to remain that way. This is shown diagrammatically in Figure 7.3.

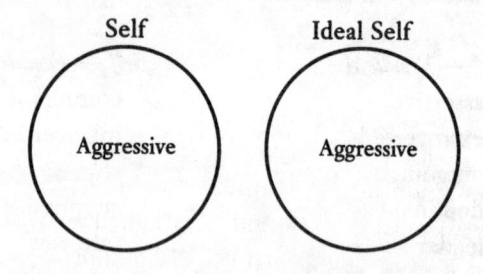

Self ─ Aggressive   Ideal Self ─ Aggressive

Figure 7.3 Unadaptive Ideal Self Objective

So, while he is high in self-esteem in this dimension, it is not adaptive. This is the same sort of problem that some criminals have. So we can have a professional thief who is happy to remain that way. He is a thief who wants to remain a thief. Here we have a thief high in self-esteem. The problem arises because this occupation leads to conflict with the law and to long terms of imprisonment. As in the case of the aggressive husband, this is not adaptive. There is clear evidence that it doesn't work well for many criminals.

Similarly, we may have a situation where the female partner in a relationship is a heavy drinker, and this is putting the relationship under great stress. In terms of Self and Ideal Self, it looks this way, as in Figure 7.4.

We might say that this woman, who is unwilling to change her heavy drinking habits, is high in self-esteem but it is ridiculous because her heavy drinking is certain to cause further problems. It is not adaptive.

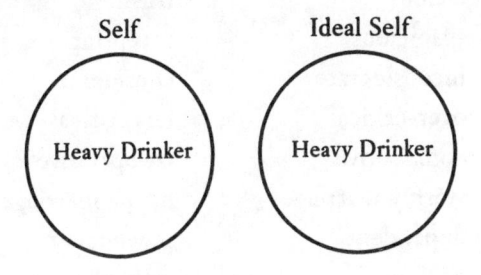

Figure 7.4 Unadaptive Ideal Self Objective

Let us look now at the process of building up our self-esteem and our power by changing ourselves toward our Ideal Self.

The first step is to take a really searching and honest look at ourselves as we are now, making sure that we include all those attributes that are preventing us from using our personal power fully, but not forgetting to list those of our other characteristics that are adaptive and helpful in our day-to-day interaction with others. In other words, we try to describe our Self as we are right now, warts and all.

The second step is to take these attributes one at a time and make a second list of what we would like to be on each of these dimensions. This is the Ideal Self, the sort of person we would like to be if we possessed the power to change ourselves in an instant.

Below is part of an actual list prepared by a male aged 26.

	Self	*Ideal Self*
	distant	friendly
	cold	warm
*	industrious	industrious
*	punctual	punctual
*	good at job	good at job
*	intelligent	intelligent
*	generous	generous

Personal Power

**	aggressive	assertive
**	intolerant	tolerant
**	jealous	trusting
**	suspicious	accepting
**	inconsiderate	considerate
**	over-critical	less critical
**	competitive	co-operative
**	stormy marriage	happy marriage
***	dependent	independent
***	anxious	relaxed
***	uptight	calm
***	indecisive	decisive
***	heavy drinker	light drinker

The third step is look at how well the two lists match up. Of the 20 characteristics of this young man, only the five marked with one asterisk are indicative of high self-esteem, in that there is a match or congruence between how he perceives himself to be now and how he would like to be. With only one quarter of the twenty matching, this indicates a considerable degree of disharmony and low self-esteem.

A useful fourth step is to group the characteristics that fall in the angry, hostile, aggressive area. For this man there are eight characteristics marked with two asterisks. This indicates that this young man has considerable problems with anger and aggression, and needs to put a lot of work into changing towards a calmer, more relaxed and assertive person. It seems quite likely that his stormy marriage may be largely a result of his aggressive approach to life, so we have included that in the angry attributes.

The fifth step is to look for indicators of anxiety and submissiveness. In the above list, we find that he has described himself as anxious, dependent, uptight and indecisive. These are clear signs of anxiety, and the heavy drinking may be his attempt to lower his anxiety states. This group is marked with three asterisks, so anxiety is also a problem for him.

The final step is to look at the dimensions where we are what we want to be, where there is already congruence between the Self and the Ideal Self. In the above list, this young man sees himself as generous, intelligent, industrious, punctual and good at his job. Providing that he is being honest with himself, he already possesses some elements of good adjustment and high self-esteem and this will provide him with a firm foundation for the substantial changes he needs to make in other areas.

This leaves the traits of 'distant' and 'cold', which might be related to his fear of failure and thus to anxiety, or they may be part of his aggressive way of relating to others. Therefore he would need to think this through to see how he would go about making changes in these two traits.

The point about the above list is that it is helpful for us to identify the emotional basis of our problem areas if we are to succeed in changing. There is no way, for example, that this young man can fix his stormy marriage if he doesn't do something about the attitudes that underlie his anger, hostility and aggression and, to a lesser degree, those that underlie his anxiety.

Of course, it is possible, and indeed very likely, that his wife has personality traits and habits that also contribute to the breakdown of their relationship. This is not the point. All we can do is to change our own ways of interacting with others. We have no power to change those people.

In looking at our Ideal Self, we need to be careful not to include impossible attributes, characteristics or situations. While we all may wish to be sensible, tolerant and calm, many of us need to look closely at our pattern of abilities so we don't include occupations for which we do not have the ability or the temperament. Not all of us are suited to be salespeople, mechanics, teachers, computer programmers or medical practitioners. Few of us have the ability to amass fortunes from small beginnings. Of course, the Ideal Self can be changed to meet changing circumstances. The important thing is for us to identify quite clearly what our present Self is like, and, as of that moment, what we would like to be.

Choosing between the Normative and the Non-Normative Approaches

The normative approach stresses conformity to what the majority of people, at any given point in time, think is appropriate and proper. Thus, anyone who diverges too markedly from the norm in either direction is, by definition, abnormal. The term abnormal carries strong overtones of sickness, whereas all it really means is 'different'. This is easy to see on a dimension such as height, where people who are extremely tall (say above two metres) or extremely short (say below one metre) are not thought of as being ill. Transfer the scale to the happy–sad dimension and divergence from the normal range carries implications of sickness. Someone who is extremely happy is called manic, and someone extremely sad is called depressed. While these departures from the norm may indeed point to psychological disturbance, the norms themselves shift from time to time, so someone who is deemed to be abnormal in one decade may be judged to be normal in the next. For example, men who openly displayed the positive emotions of love and affection in public a decade ago might have been classified as effeminate and therefore as poorly adjusted. With the current move towards recognising the crucial nature of the overt display of kindness and affection in human relationships, a different assessment might be made today.

Not so many years ago, the notion of a male being a housekeeper and rearing the children while his wife earned an income was, for most, unacceptable. While still far from the norm today, such concepts are accepted in many parts of society, even if they are still vigorously rejected by others. The point of view taken here is that there is a great deal of evidence to suggest that those who diverge from the norms of society and who are unhappy when they are forced to accept the normal situation, should adopt the non-normative approach, providing it is to their advantage and therefore an adaptive solution. For those who wish to increase their personal power, acceptance of the non-normative approach seems to be an essential ingredient.

Characteristics for Good Adjustment and High Self-Esteem

Recent research has challenged the way that society readily accepts some characteristics and roles as being necessary for female adjustment, and others as necessary for male adjustment. This recent work suggests that *well-adjusted men and women appear to share the same characteristics that are a mixture of what are usually deemed to be male and female characteristics*. This mixture includes being assertive, strong, dependable and direct on the one hand, along with being calm, kind, considerate, supportive and affectionate on the other, but does not include being aggressive, dominating or submissive.

This research fits our ideas about power like a glove, because high self-esteem in both women and men is seen to depend on the same factors, unlike the normative approach where certain characteristics are deemed to be appropriate for females and others for males. There is still a tendency for some men in our society to look down on males who are courteous, kind and considerate, and the former maintain their 'manly' image by being aggressive and dominant. Yet it is the calm, considerate ones who are coping better.

Somewhere along the line, something has gone wrong. Men are often trained to be aggressive, females to be submissive, and neither is adaptive. High levels of adjustment seem to be related to the possession and display of all the positive emotions such as consideration, gratitude, kindness, love and affection. That is, adjustment is correlated not with an aggressive attitude but with an assertive approach where people use their power sensibly to size up situations, decide what to do, and take action to protect their rights and feelings while simultaneously being considerate of the rights and feelings of others.

The main thing about this chapter is that, like the young man we have just described, we can adopt this non-normative method of looking at self-esteem, we can stop being conformists, we can begin to take charge of our own lives and start the process of using our own power in a constructive manner. We need to stop being dependent on our parents, our partners, and other people and learn to be independent, fully functioning adults. To help us make the sensible decisions and to do more sensible things in our own new solution-centred method of living, however, we need to ensure that we also have an effective method of handling issues and problems in every area of our lives; and that is the subject of the next chapter.

chapter 8
Finding Solutions

This chapter is concerned with coping with the stresses of life, with day-to-day events, and with the decisions and choices we have to make as we go about earning a living, bringing up children, making friends, deciding where to go on a holiday, and an infinite number of other things.

Some of us are expert at finding solutions to our problems, most of us are average, and some of us make a mess of things fairly often or avoid making decisions as frequently as we can. All of us can improve our performance and some of us need to improve a great deal. There are many techniques and systems that have been advanced to help us with our problem-solving skills. We have selected one that best seems to fit the idea of increasing our personal power by working on the emotional side of our lives, and particularly on those emotions that are connected with the misuse and abuse of our power.

The system we have chosen is a variant of a scheme popularised by Gordon. The system has six steps.
1. orientation to the problem
2. defining the problem
3. generation of many options
4. selection of the best option
5. putting your choice into action
6. assessing the success of your action

Step 1: Orientation to the Problem

Our orientation is the way we approach problems. It consists of the beliefs, attitudes and habits that we bring into the situation with which we have to deal. To a large degree, all of the previous chapters are about changing our orientation towards life. We have examined some of the factors that lead to an angry, hostile and aggressive approach, and looked at the evidence that shows how this leads to an abuse of our personal power and how inevitably it brings us into conflict with many with whom we interact. We now know that when we lose our cool, we frequently make bad decisions and say and do things we may later regret. We just become worse at finding solutions if our orientation is one of anger.

Similarly, we have seen that anxiety, fear and nervousness get in the road of our search for sensible solutions, and often lead to indecision, procrastination, and giving our power away to others. Let's now look at some of the areas where we can improve our orientation.

Remain Calm

It is startlingly clear that a major factor in developing the right orientation to solving our problems is keeping calm. We can't do this if we retain our old attitudes that life is about winning and getting our own way or about pleasing others. We can't do this if we live in the future or the past. We have to adopt an attitude that stresses the importance of remaining in the present because this is the only time zone where we can make an impact and solve our problems.

When we keep cool instead of getting angry, depressed, enraged or full of anxiety, we are more likely to attack the issue logically instead of becoming emotional, illogical or impulsive.

Be Confident About Being Able to Cope

When facing a problem or trying to reach a decision, it is a good idea to start with the attitude that somehow or other we will come up with a sensible solution to the issue, no matter how difficult it might appear. If it proves to be beyond our level of competence, we may need to seek help, but however we go about it, we need to feel sure that we will come up with a reasonable answer.

On the other hand, if we begin with feelings of inadequacy and of helplessness, we are unlikely to reach a sensible decision, and are very likely to fail to cope. Remember, we all have enormous personal power; it's just a matter of harnessing it. Not one of us is helpless or hopeless. We need to be confident that, somehow or another, we will cope.

Protect Your Rights and Feelings

In the previous chapter we saw that in the process of beginning to use our power constructively, it was necessary to build up our sense of self-esteem by changing various aspects of our make-up and by moving 'Self as I am now' toward 'Ideal Self as I would like to be'. However, unless we protect our basic rights and feelings, this movement will be impossible. But in order to do this, we have to know what these basic rights are. They apply to everyone irrespective of their age, gender, occupation, race or religion. A few of our rights are listed below:

1. the right to be treated as a normal member of society, and not as something strange, abnormal or inferior
2. the right to protect our feelings
3. the right to be treated with respect
4. the right to ask for something we want
5. the right to make mistakes
6. the right to say 'no' and not feel guilty
7. the right to ask for help
8. the right to take time out to think
9. the right to be as happy as possible and to feel good about ourselves
10. the right to refuse to do our best at all times
11. the right to say 'I don't know'
12. the right to be satisfied with less than a perfect solution
13. the right to change our minds
14. the right to privacy
15. the right to be kept informed about everything that affects us or may affect our lives

These rights belong to us. They are not rights we have to earn or win. They are not things that are given to us by other people. Our rights are not given to us by our parents or our partner and no one has the right to take them from us. We should not, under normal circumstances, give our rights away to others or allow them to take them from us. If we do, we lose ourselves.

This area of rights is so important that it is worth discussing each right in some detail.

Right 1 We all vary in height, weight, colour of hair and eyes; we vary in our capacity to pass examinations and tests; we vary in our capacity to listen to the opinions of others; in fact, we vary in every dimension of human activity. Some of us are perhaps more fortunate than others because, by chance, we inherit genes that enable us to run faster than others or to cope easily with scholastic tasks. This does not mean we are superior people. We are just different. Perhaps we are not very good at fixing things with our hands or relating to strangers. Does this mean we are inferior people? Of course not. We are just different.

The problem is that many of us have been exposed to situations early in our lives where we learn to feel strange, abnormal and inferior. Perhaps our parents often put us down or compared us unfavourably with a brother or sister who was better-looking or better at passing examinations. Perhaps because we were female rather than male we were given less praise, less help and were regarded as second-rate.

Let us accept that society and its members are often unfair and unjust. This does not mean that we have to accept society's assessment of us as being abnormal, second-rate citizens or inferior beings. *We are not. We are just different.* In fact, it is likely that we will have some skills, attributes or personality characteristics that may be of great use to us in coping with our lives.

The point is that we cannot afford to accept others' assessment of us as someone who is strange, abnormal or inferior. We are not second-rate citizens, and we do not have to accept such an evaluation from our parents, our partners, our employers or anyone else. *We have a right to be different, and a right to be treated as a normal member of society regardless of our educational level, our race, our gender and so on.* It is up to us to protect this right.

Rights 2 and 3 Every one of us has the right to protect our feelings so that we don't become hurt, humiliated or upset by others' words or actions. Unfortunately, it seems to be true that the ones who are most likely to trample on our feelings and to treat us with disrespect are those closest to us. It is our parents, partners, children and other family members who are most likely to abuse us in one way or another, and these are the ones we must stand up to.

Normally, our friends are much more prone to treat us with respect, but sometimes they too get out of line and we need to take charge of the situation and refuse to allow them to hurt our feelings and trample on our rights.

Right 4 Everybody has wants and everyone has the right to express these wants clearly and directly. An important part of using our power constructively is being able to communicate with one another so that we know exactly where others stand and they know how we stand. However, many people seem to expect others to read their minds or they express their wants and desires in such vague and indefinite ways that others cannot know, with any certainty, what the position really is. In the following remarks, we can see the difference between the calm assertion of a want, and an aggressive and a submissive version.

(i) 'I want you to stop raking up the past, because the money I lost can't be recovered, and talking about it only upsets us both. I want to concentrate on making our present lives happy.' This is an assertive statement, which says quite clearly what the individual wants and gives a reason for it. It is done calmly, and lets the other person know what the problem is without attacking him or her.

(ii) 'You really are a pain in the neck the way you are always throwing the past in my face. Why don't you shut up about that money or I'll leave.' This is an aggressive way of handling the situation, which probably won't solve the problem of raking up the past, but which will almost certainly make the other person resentful and perhaps cause further problems.

(iii) 'All this talk is upsetting me. I think I'll go to the library.' This is a non-assertive way of trying to cope. It leaves the other person in doubt about what is actually upsetting us. Withdrawing from the situation by going to the library leaves no chance for the problem to be clarified.

When we want something, it is best to say it clearly, directly and honestly. Then we have a good chance of success. Here are some examples.

- 'It would be terrific if you would visit me more often.'
- 'I feel that I am not being consulted about managing our finances. From now on, I would appreciate it if you would involve me in all financial decisions.'
- 'I want you to stop criticising me all the time. If what I am doing is harmful or likely to hurt someone else, then criticism is OK, but your constant complaints about even trivial issues are unnecessary. Please think about this and try to avoid being over-critical.'

Right 5 No matter how expert we become at coping with the problems that face us, we will make mistakes from time to time and *we have a right to make mistakes without being blamed, accused or being made to feel guilty*. An appropriate response to making a mistake is to say: 'Stiff luck. I got it wrong. I'll try again'.

Right 6 Many of us believe that when a friend or a member of the family asks for help, we must say 'yes' because we should help this person. Generally speaking, we try to help as often as possible, but we have a right to say 'no' when it conflicts with other priorities. We have a limited amount of time and energy, and if we say 'yes' to everything and everyone, our lives become a mess. It is not selfish to say 'no' if that is in our best interests when we have looked at all the demands being made upon us.

Close friends may get a little hurt if we refuse a request, but it is in their interests as well as ours not to agree to do something we don't want to do, because we would resent it, and them.

Right 7 Most of us are inclined to be over-cautious about asking other people for help. Generally, we should try to become as self-sufficient as possible, but there are some situations and events that we find difficult because we don't have enough experience or ability. In these situations, it is wise to ask for help from those who are most likely to be able to deal with the problem. Many people, in fact, feel flattered when asked to help in areas where they are competent. Of course, they have the right to say 'no' and if they do, we should accept this and seek help elsewhere without resenting a refusal.

Right 8 Many people want us to make instant decisions when there is really no overwhelming urgency. Insist upon your right to take time out to examine the options available to you, so that you are less likely to make the wrong decision. When someone says 'I need an answer right now' it usually means 'fairly soon'. If you say 'Look, I want to think this through. I'll get back to you later today as soon as I've reached a decision', this will usually be accepted. Agreeing to go on a holiday with someone with whom you really wouldn't feel at ease, or when it would cut across other commitments, is often done under much pressure. Agreeing to join an organisation, or to go to a party when you really don't want to, can be avoided by taking a brief time out to think about whether you really do want to agree.

Right 9 Many of us don't feel we have a right to be happy or say to ourselves 'I'm really a nice sort of person'. Everybody has this right, no matter how bad the past has been, provided a concentrated effort is being made to succeed in the present. We should not wallow in self-pity or feelings of guilt. We should try to make the present as happy as possible for ourselves and make the lives of those close to us happy as well.

Right 10 The right to refuse to do our best at all times is a variation of saying 'no' without feeling guilty. If someone asks us to help, we may just say 'no' or we may compromise and say 'Well, I can't help all day, but I'll help for two hours in the morning'.

Right 11 There is no reason in the world why we should know everything, so there is nothing to be ashamed of in saying 'I don't know'. If you are really interested or curious about the issue, you may want to find out the answer to the question, but often the best thing is to suggest to the questioner where to find out the answer. If not, leave it at 'Sorry, I don't know'. We don't have to provide an answer to every query.

Right 12 Perfect solutions to problems are rare. Compromises on some issues will have to be reached. This compromise is usually between protecting our rights and being considerate of the rights of others. Despite this, some people feel that anything less than getting their own way is a failure.

Right 13 The right to change our minds is really a variation of our right to make mistakes. If we make a decision about how to act and then find we have made a mistake, or if fresh evidence or other factors not previously considered become available, we have the right to change our mind. Unfortunately, once some people have made a decision, they become stubborn and stick to it even when there is clear evidence that they have made a mistake and that it would be a good idea for them to change their minds.

Right 14 All of us have the right to have time and space to ourselves. Time taken to meditate and think about issues seems to be essential. Usually, this involves withdrawing to a private space where we are unlikely to be interrupted. Sometimes, less well-adjusted people will resent these activities of those close to them. Clear and honest communication about the necessity for privacy becomes compelling.

Right 15 In many relationships, a dominating partner will use devices such as secrecy to get his or her own way. Similarly, an anxious, submissive person may use secrecy to avoid issues. Both result in a breakdown in communication. For example, the dominant partner may keep income details from the other, so that he or she can indulge in gambling. Another anxious person facing redundancy might keep this information secret, fearing rejection and condemnation. Both partners of these people have the right to know about anything that affects their future. If the partner of the gambler were to find out half of the income is being gambled away he or she may get resentful, and clearly it is essential that the partner of the worker facing redundancy be informed that their income is under threat.

Often, this secrecy is hidden under the guise of protecting the partner from unpleasant news. This rationalisation usually means that the person who knows about the issue is afraid to speak about it, and selfishly keeps it secret.

Step 2: Defining the Problem

Some problems are quite clear-cut and fully defined from the beginning. If an eleven-year-old says 'Mum, I want to get my ears pierced so I can wear these earrings', there is no doubt what the situation is. At the other extreme, a wife who has recently returned to part-time work and has joined an environmental group comes home after being at a meeting to find her husband apparently asleep in bed. The next day he speaks to her in monosyllables and then only when asked a direct question. The silent treatment is on, leaving the source of the problem quite unclear to her. She thinks that perhaps she might not be helping enough with the children's homework or perhaps he has got the sack and is afraid to tell her.

Now, *unless the problem is sorted out and defined quite precisely, it is unlikely to be solved*. In this case, the definition of the problem might proceed as follows. Quite clearly the wife has a right to know what the problem is. She has to assert herself, so she might say, 'Bob, you seem to be very unhappy, and I don't know why. Since I arrived home last night you have barely spoken to me, and you haven't touched or kissed me, and that makes me unhappy. I want you to tell me what the problem is so that we can sort it out together'.

'Look, Sue, our whole life is a mess.'

'What do you mean? Tell me specifically what it is that's upsetting you.'

'Well, we never seem to have much time together any more. We don't go anywhere together or talk to anyone, and I'm sick of it.'

'Is it my work or my night meetings with the environmental crowd creating the problem?'

'I think the work part is OK, but every time I want to speak to you at night, the phone rings and you have long conversations about dams and forests, and I feel shut out. I don't seem to be part of your life any more.'

'I didn't know you felt so strongly about my environmental commitment. How about if I cut down my committee work from three nights a week to one? That will reduce the phone calls, and we will have more time to talk. How about if you come with me on the one night I do go?'

After further discussion, the nature of the problem is totally clarified and the outcome is as follows: Bob joins Sue's environmental group, and eventually becomes very involved. It also emerges that Bob likes going out to dinner occasionally and likes jazz concerts. They agree that they can use the two nights formerly given over to meetings to enjoy these activities. Sue also asks him not to bottle up his feelings in future, and to speak honestly and directly to her about them. Bob agrees to try, so the immediate problem is fixed, and future benefits also become a possibility.

A quite different problem faces Jean who notices that her husband, Harry, appears to be losing his interest in sex. Jean becomes quite apprehensive about the situation, thinking that he might be having an affair with another woman, that he might be depressed, that he might be becoming impotent and many other possible reasons. She tries all sorts of remedies with no success. Finally, she decides to ask him quite directly what the problem is.

Harry has been a successful tax consultant, with a large number of firms and individuals as clients. Recently, he has decided to try working with a large multinational corporation. During the conversation with Jean, he admits he has made a mistake about changing his job and says that he wants to return to his former one-man business. Jean can see that he is in conflict, and agrees that it would be a good idea for him to leave the corporation. It soon emerges that Harry could not bring himself to ring his former clients to tell them that he was restarting his practice, because they might reject him.

Knowing now what the problem is, and feeling great relief that it is not centred on their marriage, Jean suggests that he ring his old clients to discuss the matter with them. He does this and succeeds beyond his wildest dreams, with the vast majority being only too delighted to use his efficient services again.

Jean could not solve their marital problems until the nature of the problem became clear. Basically, what appeared to be a sexual problem was in reality an occupational problem. Jean and Bob could have spent much time and money going to a sex therapist. This was not the problem. The solution was to attack the occupational one.

Step 3: Generation of Options

Having decided what a given problem is, so that it is no longer fuzzy and vague but clear-cut and definite, we have to work out what to do to solve it. The way to go about this is to *list all the options we can possibly think of without judging at this point whether they are good solutions or not.*

If we take an example of an everyday problem, we can see more clearly this need for looking at many options. A househusband with a wife and two children lives a kilometre from the shopping centre. Usually he walks there to buy supplies, but at weekends he uses the family car. In emergencies his wife uses public transport to go to work and leaves the car at home. One or both children help with the shopping during holidays, and occasionally after school.

Consider the following situation. The man checks on supplies, notices that they are running low on various articles and says to himself 'Well, I need to do some shopping urgently'. He recognises that there is a problem and makes a first attempt to define it. However, even in this mundane aspect of living, it is still not clear what action he should take to solve it. The first step is to define the elements in tangible terms. Probably in this case the phrase that needs definition is 'things are getting low'. So he makes a list, and the problem now reads 'We are low in A, B, C, ... Z. I certainly need to go shopping today'. Given his lack of transport, the problem could be refined further. 'A, C, E and F are urgent because they are needed for breakfast and cut lunches tomorrow. The remainder could wait until the week-end.' The problem is now clearly defined, and various alternative solutions can be generated.

The evidence on the generation of options suggests that the more alternatives that can be generated, the better the outcome. In the present case, the possibilities are fairly limited. Some are listed below:

1. Walk and do all the shopping.
2. Walk and get the essentials, leaving the remainder until the weekend.
3. Change the breakfast and cut-lunch requirements, and arrange with wife for use of the car the following day.
4. Ask children for help after school, and get the lot.
5. Ask children to get essentials after school.
6. Borrow essentials from neighbours.
7. Go to supermarket and ask them to deliver.
8. Hitch a ride with a neighbour.
9. Do the total shopping and ask wife to pick it up on the way home.
10. Have a showdown with wife on the need for more help with the housework.
11. Buy a second car.
12. Say it is all too much, and do nothing.
13. Any combinations of the above such as hitch a ride with a neighbour to demonstrate the need for a second car.
14. Go back to work and employ a housekeeper.
15. Decide to go back to part-time work to buy a second car in order to do the shopping.
16. Walk up, buy the lot and taxi back.

Without going any further, it is plain that many alternatives can be generated even in the simplest situations. Some of these are appropriate, some not. Decisions about these are the next step and we will return to this shortly, but let's look at two more examples first.

Consider the plight of a woman who has recently returned home from hospital after treatment for depression. For her, the problem that upset her initially and led to the depression is still there when she comes home. Her workaholic husband is still working eighteen hours a day, seven days a week. Her definition of the problem may be as follows: 'I feel depressed and lonely. The problem seems to be that my husband is always working. When he does come home, he is too tired to do anything. He flops in front of TV, has a drink and goes to bed. When I get up in the morning, he has already left for work. He rarely sees the children because he brings work home at the weekend, or goes to work. I want his support and companionship, life is boring, and the children are getting out of hand. It is highly desirable that he spend less time on work and more with the children, or the family will disintegrate. The problem is to get him to see that our marriage is failing and that I am depressed and unhappy. Now what steps can I take?'

Her list of options was as follows:

1 Confront husband, demand more of his time and threaten divorce.
2 Make a list of hours he has worked over the last fortnight, including weekends. List the number of social outings during the last few months. Document lack of communication with him, and between him and the children. Document financial position. Describe own feelings of loneliness, depression and feelings of being abandoned. Ask him what he thinks can be done to improve the situation and make specific requests for change.
3 Consult a marriage guidance counsellor.
4 Ask a friend for help.
5 Go home to mother.
6 Accept this as a woman's lot in life.
7 Ring his boss and demand that he does something.
8 Do nothing.
9 Ask him to change his job.
10 Offer to get a part-time job if he will work reasonable hours.
11 Get a full-time job to counter loneliness.

12 Take some tranquillisers.
13 Learn to play golf and keep busy.
14 Go to a solicitor and begin divorce proceedings.
15 Have a few brandies to calm down.
16 Pack a bag and go away to a seaside hotel for a week to think things over.
17 Jump off a bridge.

There are probably dozens of other options open, but at least careful thought has been given to generating a reasonable number of quite different ways of handling the situation without, at this stage, thinking about whether they are good or bad solutions.

This woman has ample time to think up a variety of solutions, but some problems require snap decisions. It is to one of these that we now turn.

Take the case of a male in a pressure-to-drink situation that arises out of the blue. He has an ulcer and has been advised to avoid alcohol altogether. He is on a plane that has just reached its cruising altitude. A friend whom he has not seen for years drops into the adjoining seat. After the usual greetings, the friend orders two drinks from a passing flight attendant without consulting him, and reopens the conversation by telling him about his current activities. As the arrival of the drinks is imminent, a quick solution to the problem has to be reached.

First, the problem has to be defined: 'This man, an old friend and drinking partner, has suddenly appeared after five years and ordered me a drink. He does not know that I have an ulcer. I don't want to hurt his feelings by refusing to drink, but I'll hurt myself and my family more if I do. What can I do?'

The alternatives he came up with were:

1 Interrupt his conversation. Tell him that you don't want the drink because you have an ulcer.
2 Wait for the drinks to arrive; do the same.
3 Interrupt and give another reason for not drinking
4 Wait and give another reason for not drinking.
5 Apologise to flight attendant and ask her to bring a soft drink instead of the whisky, and then offer explanation to friend.

6   Abuse the friend for not having the courtesy to ask if you wanted a drink.
7   Say nothing, but don't drink the whisky.
8   Say you are not feeling well, and ask him to drink your whisky.
9   Drink the whisky, but resolve to have only one.

We will use these three situations to illustrate the next step, decision making.

Step 4: Selection of the Best Option

In deciding what to do, we make a list of all the options that might work and put them in order from best to least likely. In doing this, it is essential to bear in mind the orientation discussed earlier. As the aim is to remain calm, any angry or aggressive option has to be ruled out. Any option that allows someone else to walk over you, to hurt you, to humiliate you or to make you feel small cannot be accepted, and all the other steps have to be considered because all six sections of the problem-solving process are interrelated.

The Shopping Situation

The task here is to match the options with the problem and judge how likely each one is to solve the problem.

1   Walking up and doing all the shopping is rejected, because getting everything on the list will mean that the load is too heavy to carry.
    Decision: Reject.
2   Getting the essentials and leaving the remainder is a possibility because it will solve the problem, but it will mean two trips.
    Decision: A remote possibility.
3   Changing the breakfast and cut-lunch requirements is rejected on two counts. There are no satisfactory substitutes for some of the items, and he knows it's important for his wife to have the car the following day.
    Decision: Reject.

4 Both children are studying for exams the following week, so he decides it isn't fair to ask them for help.
   Decision: Reject.
5 Asking children to buy the essentials has the same difficulties as option 4.
   Decision: Reject.
6 His habit is to borrow from neighbours only in a real emergency, and this is not one.
   Decision: Reject.
7 The supermarket requires orders to be in before noon.
   Decision: Reject.
8 It is unclear whether any of the neighbours will be driving to the supermarket that day.
   Decision: Reject.
9 He can ring his wife to ask her to pick up all the goods on her way home, but she frequently works overtime.
   Decision: A possibility.
10 Having a showdown implies anger and aggression. It does, however, raise the possibility that he might need more help with the housework.
   Decision: A different problem. Consider later.
11 Buying another car is also a different problem.
   Decision: Consider later.
12 Doing nothing does not solve this problem and is likely to create more problems.
   Decision: Reject.
13 The need for a second car is another problem.
14 Returning to work is another problem.
15 Another problem. Same as option 14.
16 Walking up, buying the lot and getting a taxi back will solve the problem without getting help from the children and will save a second trip.
   Decision: Accept as best solution.

As a result of thinking through his problem calmly, he has arrived at a decision that will almost certainly succeed. In the unlikely event of a taxi not being available he decides to ring his wife for help (a variant of option 9). While thinking this problem through it has become clear to him that the thought of going back to work on a part-time basis and using the money to buy a second car is very attractive, so he files this away as a separate problem to be dealt with in the near future.

The Workaholic Husband

1. The first option involves a confrontation and a threat of divorce. In this form it is aggressive and threats should not be made at all, as they back you into a corner.
   Decision: Reject.
2. Describing the situation calmly, honestly and directly, and asking for full communication about the issue is usually the best way.
   Decision: Accept as best option.
3. Seeking marriage guidance is often desirable if the marriage looks like failing, but sometimes a face-to-face discussion between the partners will solve the problem.
   Decision: Accept as a good fall-back option.
4. Any friend is likely to be biased and usually does not have the skills to settle marriage problems.
   Decision: Reject.
5. Going home to mother does not solve the problem.
   Decision: Reject.
6. Accepting this as a woman's lot is ridiculous. Women have rights in marriages and need to protect these rights.
   Decision: Reject.
7. Ringing his boss and demanding that he do something is likely to antagonise the husband, who has a right to keep his private affairs confidential.
   Decision: Reject.
8. Doing nothing does not solve the problem.
   Decision: Reject.
9. Asking him to change his job might work.
   Decision: Retain as a possibility.
10. Making an offer to work part-time, in return for his working less, might work. In this case, it is not necessary

because he is earning a very large salary and really doesn't need the overtime.
Decision: Reject.

11 Working to counter loneliness will not solve the children's problems.
Decision: Reject.

12 Tranquillisers have only a temporary effect. The problem would remain.
Decision: Reject.

13 Learning to play golf might help, but the basic problem would still be there.
Decision: Reject.

14 Seeking divorce might be necessary if he refuses to change, but this seems premature.
Decision: A last-resort option.

15 Drinking alcohol might make you feel better for a while, but it is not a permanent solution.
Decision: Reject.

16 Going away for a week is not necessary. Once the options are listed, it is better to decide to act at the first favourable opportunity.
Decision: Reject.

17 Suicide would make the situation of the children even worse, and their rights are very important.
Decision: Reject out of hand.

The woman decided to face the husband (option 2) to seek marriage guidance if he refused to change (option 3) and, if necessary, to look at the need for divorce (option 14).

The Aeroplane Drink

1 Being open and honest about the ulcer and telling the friend about the dangers of his drinking alcohol sounds like the best way to go.
Decision: Accept as the best option.

2 Waiting until the drinks arrive before taking action is not a good idea. The longer the time, the harder it is to justify delay.

Decision: Reject.
3. Giving another reason for not drinking is lying.
   Decision: Reject.
4. Waiting and giving another reason for not drinking involves both delay and a lie.
   Decision: Reject.
5. Asking the flight attendant to change the order is a good option if the flight attendant has disappeared and returns with the drink before option 1 can be implemented.
   Decision: Accept as best option if option 1 cannot be used.
6. Abusing people is aggressive behaviour which, in this case, would almost certainly lose him a friend who at the worst has been a little thoughtless and discourteous.
   Decision: Reject.
7. Saying nothing, but not drinking, leaves him with the new problem of disposing of the drink.
   Decision: Reject.
8. Saying he is not feeling well is lying.
   Decision: Reject.
9. Swallowing the drink is ridiculous, people-pleasing behaviour. It will make him ill.
   Decision: Reject.

The man put option 1 into operation and everything went off smoothly. The friend changed the order, and the conversation flowed on.

These three cases serve to illustrate how the orientation and the generation of options usually lead to a sensible decision on what to do to solve the problem. Wherever possible, fall-back options should be chosen in case the first doesn't work. For the woman with the workaholic husband, it would probably have been better if she had included in her decision a further clause. 'If he reacts badly, I'll drop it and allow a few days to pass before I return to the subject. This will give him time to think about what I have said and perhaps he will then be prepared to discuss the situation.'

Step 5: Putting the Decision into Action

This is assertion, which is discussed in the next chapter. It is useless working out what to do if, when the time comes, we do nothing. That means we allow other people to trample on our rights without even letting them know what they are doing. This is actually showing a lack of respect for the rights of others, who have the right to know about conditions and circumstances that concern them.

People fail to act because they are afraid of getting hurt emotionally, and sometimes physically. They also fail to act because they are afraid of upsetting others and for various other reasons. Even if the decision turns out to be wrong, it is better to act than do nothing because it gives others the chance to ask for clarification, and at least lets others know how you feel.

Step 6: Assessing the Success of Your Action

Quite simply, this is just looking at the result of putting a decision into action. There are many possible outcomes, a few of which need special consideration.

Complete Failure

If the action does not solve the problem, at least we have done our best. The best thing we can do is to accept the situation as a new problem to be solved, and to start again. It is possible that we have failed to take account of critical factors. For example, there is reason to suspect that the workaholic we described earlier had ceased to love his wife and was only remaining in the marriage because he was worried about what his business partners would say about a divorce. If she had acted, this fact might have emerged and divorce might have become the first option in the revision of the problem.

Complete Success

No problems. This will increase your sense of self-esteem and make it more likely that you will handle that sort of situation well if it crops up again.

Partial Success

Compromise solutions are frequently the best we can achieve. This may come about because, in the original appraisal of the situation, we overlook an important element or fail to see that the rights of others are being infringed. Perfect solutions are rare, and many people fail because they feel that perfect solutions can always be found.

Sometimes, of course, we may be able to go back after a partial success and try something else to improve the situation further.

Generation of New Problems

Free and full discussion of any issue frequently generates new areas for discussion. In his assessment of the options in the shopping problem, the househusband came to realise that he wanted to go back to work and decided to use the money to buy a second car. His wife pointed out that it would also be necessary to get some domestic help — a new problem to be solved.

We are now in a position where we know how to build up our self-esteem and have a method of attacking our day-to-day problems to add to our understanding of the nature of personal power. We also have a firm basis for constructing a method of coping with the immense variety of issues, problems and events that we face each day.

One way of looking at life is to see it as just an endless chain of events with which we have to deal, one at a time in the best way we can. Even in a single day we have to make hundreds, even thousands of decisions. Most of these decisions are routine ones that we make without much thought; others are very simple to solve but a few may be very difficult because the best solution is not at all obvious.

It begins when we wake up. Our first decision may be whether to get out of bed or not, the second decision may be what to have for breakfast. These two are probably easy. The third may be how to respond to a child who won't get out of bed or who is rude. This may not be so simple. And so it goes on. If we get the first decision right and get out of bed, we may already feel a bit better.

If we handle the rude child firmly and well without losing our cool, we will certainly feel good about ourselves. If, during the day, we handle ourselves well in the vast majority of cases, at the end of the day we can look back and say 'Yes, I've had a great day. Even when I made a mistake at work, I promptly admitted it and went back and fixed it up; I've been pleasant to my family and to my fellow workers and considerate of their rights and feelings. But when my partner tried to get me to agree to something I thought was not a good idea, I worked out a better strategy and calmly but firmly went about convincing him to change his mind'.

When we have one good day, the chances are that we'll sleep well and wake up refreshed and begin the next day in a good frame of mind, so we are even more likely to have another successful day. It all comes down to remaining calm, staying in the present, and concentrating on making good decisions, one by one. Seen this way, life is not all that difficult. All we have to do is to solve one little problem at a time.

chapter 9
Being Assertive

The bulk of this book has been given over to what we hope is a convincing argument that those of us who abuse our personal power by resorting to anger in its various forms and by expressing that anger aggressively will almost inevitably find ourselves in conflict with others in our personal, family, social, sporting and business lives. Inevitably, we become isolated as these others avoid us. We have also shown there is a very close causal connection between angry, aggressive behaviour and early death from strokes and heart attacks. These ways of behaving have been labelled as Type A behaviour.

We have also concentrated on showing that somewhat the same effects can occur to those of us who are into keeping the peace at any price, and into pleasing others by misuse of our personal power. Those of us who are anxious and submissive doormats, who worry most of the time about the future and who live in dread that those around us will withdraw their love and approval, are misusing our personal power. As well as the chaos that results in our marital, social and business lives, we have shown that once again there is a close connection between this anxiety and fear on the one hand and increased blood pressure, strokes and heart disease on the other. Additionally, it has been made clear that high levels of anxiety predispose us to the use of tranquillisers and alcohol and, of course, to addiction to these substances. We have labelled these ways of behaving as Type X behaviour.

The alternative to both Type A and Type X behaviour has been labelled as Type B. This is an altogether totally different way of living and entails ridding ourselves of many of our old habits, attitudes and beliefs, and wholeheartedly adopting a completely new set of habits, attitudes and beliefs.

Fortunately, Type B behaviour can be used in developing a new method of coping, which we can use in all spheres of our life where we not only protect our basic rights but simultaneously consider the rights and feelings of those around us, whether they be family members, friends, acquaintances, business associates or rivals in the sporting arena.

As we have already stated, the most effective way to protect our rights is to become assertive. Assertiveness involves remaining calm, stating our wants and expressing our feelings honestly, directly and appropriately. It also involves taking into consideration the rights and feelings of others, and very importantly, it includes the expression of positive feelings, such as kindness, gratitude, affection and love.

Assertiveness involves:
1. putting our problem-solving choice of option into action
2. protecting our own rights and feelings
3. considering the rights and feelings of others
4. expressing positive emotions toward others
5. expressing wants and feelings honestly, directly and appropriately
6. being calm
7. living in the present
8. doing the best we can

The motive for assertiveness is to communicate ideas, feelings and desires to others so that problems can be clarified and solved through full and free discussion. Many people believe that the purpose of life is to get their own way at all times and to win every argument, and that the best way to achieve these aims is to be very aggressive. To gain their objectives, they are prepared to hurt, to humiliate and to alienate others.

Aggression involves:
1. putting our case by raising our voices, yelling and demanding in an angry manner
2. ignoring the rights and feelings of others
3. trying to achieve our goals at the expense of others
4. closing off communication
5. alienating others
6. being angry
7. living in the past
8. needing to win at all costs

The motive for aggression is to dominate, to hurt and to humiliate others to gain one's own ends. Aggression is aimed at stopping communication and preventing an examination of options that don't please the aggressor. The way of behaving that many others frequently adopt is to be non-assertive or submissive.

Non-assertive or submissive behaviour involves:
1. Being so overly concerned about what others think of us, about hurting their feelings, about pleasing them, that we fail to act on what we have decided to do, or do something that is unlikely to solve the problem well
2. failing to protect our rights and feelings
3. allowing others to hurt and humiliate us
4. ending up feeling miserable and depressed
5. being anxious
6. living in the future
7. avoiding decision making
8. perfectionist behaviour

The motive underlying non-assertive and submissive behaviour is to please others or to avoid their displeasure. It rarely works, as they end up losing respect for us, become irritated and disgusted, and feel pity for us. *Our wants and feelings are not communicated, so discussion is restricted.*

Another problem we have found with anxious people early in the change period, is their tendency to confuse assertiveness with aggression. So, in our attempt to change, we often become angry and aggressive. If we look at the section preceding this paragraph we can see that, in order to be assertive, we have to be calm, laid-back and relaxed, but firmly resolved to put forward our point of view. Our motive is to communicate rather than primarily to get our own way. We should be prepared to change our minds if, during the discussion, we are convinced that we are wrong. Equating assertiveness with being firm instead of being compliant may be a good way of looking at the issue and of preventing ourselves from moving towards the angry, aggressive Type A, instead of maintaining our firm and calm Type B behaviour.

Do We Need to Change?

From time to time we have asked you to fill in questionnaires, to score them and to work out your personal level of functioning in these areas by comparing your scores with others of the same sex and about the same age as you. Each of these levels on the various measures of different aspects of anger, anxiety and job stress was rated as Low, Low Average, Average, High Average, or High.

Any score that puts your personal level as High or Very High is a clear and reliable indicator that you urgently need to begin working on your anger, hostility and aggression, or on your anxiety, fear and submissiveness, or all of these, and to begin to change towards becoming more relaxed, calm and co-operative through practising being more assertive.

Even scores rated as Average indicate that there is work to be done. This is because the average person in our society is almost certainly far too angry and aggressive in their relationships with others. They may also be adversely affected by an Average level of anxiety.

In summary, any score other than one rated as Low or Low Average should be treated with concern and taken as indicating a need to change. Any High or Very High score should be taken seriously and used to galvanise you into action. If your anger scores are High or Very High, it would be wise to read again the chapters about the abuse of power and about how to change your attitudes and behaviour. High or Very High anxiety levels also show the need to re-read the sections about anxiety reduction.

If you are still having difficulty after six to nine months or so, and these emotions are still causing significant problems in your life, you may need to seek professional help.

Remember, you cannot become perfect in any of these areas, although we should seek to get as close to that as we can. The aim is to stop abusing and misusing our power and to learn to use it constructively. We can make really significant progress towards that goal in a relatively short space of time, provided we accept the need to work as hard as we can at achieving that aim.

Can We Change?

Many of the men and women who have successfully responded to counselling about changing their Type A behaviour initially made claims such as: 'My grandfather was angry, my mother was angry and so am I. This is the way I am, and there's no way in the world that I can change'. Implicitly, this is an argument that anger and aggression are inherited traits like the colour of our eyes, our height and our skin colour. In fact, the evidence from many areas of research points to the opposite interpretation. Anger might certainly be a normal, natural emotion but we are not born with the habit of responding to criticism with anger; we are not born with the habit of getting hot under the collar when a colleague is promoted instead of us; we are not born with a habit of losing our temper when we make a mistake. Indeed, as we grow up, we may learn to attach our feelings of anger to more and more classes of events and gradually build up a wide variety of angry, aggressive responses to these events.

Some of us are fortunate in that, by the luck of the draw, we have parents who are wise and emotionally mature. These parents may teach us from the beginning that anger and aggression are not acceptable and that there are better ways of handling criticism, our careers and our mistakes. By the time these fortunate ones reach adulthood, they will have learned to handle these areas in a calm, relaxed and laid-back manner. Do they occasionally fly off the handle and lose control? Of course they do. No one is perfect, and no one will ever be perfect. But for them these occasions are rare, and because of their strong habit of keeping cool, the outburst is usually short-lived and little lasting harm is done as they quickly recognise the folly of such behaviour. They readily admit that they have gone wrong, make amends and get back on track again.

Some of us are less fortunate in that we are exposed to experiences early in our lives that set us on a path where various forms of anger and aggression dominate our existence or where we build up a pattern wherein we frequently respond with high levels of anxiety. We may have had a dominating parent or parents, parents who were over-protective, or we may have been physically abused or continually put down. We may even have lost our parents in early childhood or been the victim of rape or incest. No matter how disastrous our past has been, we still have the power to change. Earlier in this book we described the seminal work of Friedman and his associates in training men and women who had had at least one heart attack, to change from Type A to Type B ways of living. Their success in doing so proves conclusively that it can be done and done in a relatively short time. But, you may argue, this only occurred when these men and women reached a crisis point where it was change or die. This is true. But it does not affect the argument at all. If we are sufficiently motivated, we can change ourselves at any point in time.

We want to argue that the best time to change is now. Don't wait until your loved one leaves you; don't wait for a heart attack. Don't choose to remain in a state of misery or despair. Use your immense power to change now.

The argument we are putting forward is that we should all take a good hard look at ourselves. We have produced arguments to prove that being angry, hostile and aggressive doesn't work, and that anxiety, fear and submissiveness produce the same results. We are silent when we should speak up, we take refuge in perfectionism and become indecisive. Either way, the result is chaos.

Why wait for a health crisis to occur before we change? Why wait for a domestic crisis? Why wait until we resort to alcohol or tranquillisers to make us feel better? We don't need a crisis to come to a head before we decide to change. We have the power to change whenever we decide to. Don't procrastinate. Start now!

chapter 10
Using Our Power Constructively

Using our power constructively by being assertive involves taking control of our own lives in a firm, decisive but calm way. It entails accepting that we are responsible for everything we say, for everything we do and for our own emotional well-being. No longer can we lean on others and allow them to make decisions for us. Emotional dependency is out. From now on, we have to resolve not to allow anyone, and especially those closest to us, to push us around, to control us, to manipulate us or to dominate us in any way. Above all, it involves changing those underlying motives, attitudes, habits and beliefs that in the past have prevented us from acting in the assertive ways that allow us to cooperate with others, to improve our communication, to make sensible decisions and to do sensible things. Let us begin by looking at how assertiveness works in our close relationships.

In Australia, the rate of divorce and separation has reached 43 per cent and is still climbing. In the USA the equivalent figure is over 50 per cent. If we were to add to these figures a guess at the number of marriages and de facto relationships that remain intact but are characterised by constant argument and bickering, by violence and cruelty, by excessive use of alcohol and other drugs and by many other indicators of breakdown, we would probably find that no more than 33 per cent of all relationships are happy, rewarding and fulfilling for both partners.

Now if Toyota, Ford and General Motors Holden produced only one vehicle in three that worked, the chances of these companies staying in business would be very low. If we had a telephone that worked efficiently once in three times, we would soon change to another service provider where the quality control provided us with a reliable instrument. If we had a refrigerator that only worked every third day, we would soon rid ourselves of it in favour of another make or model that gave us the consistent, dependable service we demand.

There are, of course, many differences between industries and companies that sell us cars, telephones and refrigerators on the one hand, and close relationships of all kinds on the other. One major difference is that in marriage we don't have to rely on the quality of the managing director of any board to create working policies and reforms; we don't have to rely on middle management and the workforce to put these policies and reforms into operation. When it comes to relationships, we are in charge of our own destiny. We can sit down with our partner and calmly discuss what policies we need to implement so that our own relationship will not only survive but will provide the love, affection, feelings of security and happiness that are to be found in close relationships that are working well. We are in charge! It is our own responsibility to work out the policies and reforms. It is our own responsibility to put these policies and reforms into practice and to make sure that they work. We are in charge of our own destiny here, depending only on ourselves and one other human being.

And there's the rub. Only with the total co-operation and good will of one other human being can we make this project viable. The good news, of course, is that we are also in charge of the selection process. We choose our own partners, whereas we usually have little or no say in the selection of the board of a huge industry. Two is a manageable number, so close relationships have a head start over a big public company. Impromptu meetings can be called without notice, and the two partners are much more likely to be aware of the emotional state of their partner and of his or her needs than will the comparative strangers on most boards. More generally, we all have the power to work co-operatively to ensure that our close relationships thrive and flourish.

The other side of this coin is that the emotional investment of the partners in close relationships can and does lead to anger, hostility and aggression or to anxiety and submissiveness, all of which play a large part in the erosion of co-operation and lead to a breakdown in communication. This is what this book has been all about: if we want good relationships, we have to work hard at changing ourselves, at abandoning the old ideas, attitudes and beliefs and at building up new habits, attitudes and beliefs. This will enable us to interact co-operatively with our partner, to foster free, open and honest communication and to keep these communication lines open at all times.

Perhaps one of the reasons for the low success rate in marriage and other close relationships is that very few of us are prepared to look hard at our relationship and to work hard at it in the same way that we are prepared to invest huge amounts of our time and energy thinking about work, seeking promotion and advancement, formulating policies and devising ways of implementing these policies in our occupations. We just fall in love, form a relationship and expect it to work. We make ad hoc decisions on the run; even if a policy decision is jointly made, it is usually quietly forgotten by one partner and left entirely to the other to implement because one partner is too busy making money to be concerned with such 'trivia'.

Obviously then, the first step in establishing a relationship that is likely to last, and to work in the fullest sense of that word, is for both partners to come to an agreement that their relationship is to be the primary focus. If this doesn't work, nothing else will. It seems unlikely that two people can have a happy life together if their relationship is strained, because this strain will spread to every area of their life.

So the first step in being assertive for those of us who are fortunate enough to have a close relationship is to sit down with our partner and make a commitment to work hard to make the relationship change and grow. Fortunately, we have the power to do this. All we need is the will.

While this is not a marriage manual, a brief look at some of the factors that are critical in the success or failure of a relationship will highlight the ways in which assertive behaviour can provide an atmosphere in which relationships can flourish, and simultaneously demonstrate how the abuse or misuse of our power will undermine and ultimately destroy these relationships.

The Signs of a Good Relationship

Let's take marriage and similar partnerships first. As suggested earlier, there are two sets of factors in a close relationship that need to be considered. The first set comes about because in a satisfactory relationship, the partners will like spending time with one another dealing with their day-to-day activities. In this sense, a marriage is like a close friendship or a business partnership. If for the moment we see it as a business partnership, then certain things will follow. A marriage, however, has elements over and above this. If it is to work, there also has to be continuing love and affection openly expressed. There will also be a sexual relationship, which is important, and there may be children to bring up, educate and set loose to function as independent, mature adults. This set of factors is the one that obviously is critical for the success of the relationship, but it is interwoven and inextricably mixed with the partnership factors. Many close relationships, including marriages, that finish on the rocks founder not only because of the absence of love and affection but because the first and more mundane partnership elements are never worked out.

Perhaps the best way to look at marriage and other close relationships is to look at these partnership aspects first. There seem to be at least six areas that are absolutely essential for a business partnership to work, and all of these apply to close relationships. To provide ourselves with an optimum setting in which our marriages and other close relationships can thrive and grow we need to:

1. Change to a co-operative way of living and practise being co-operative at all times and under all circumstances.
2. Do nothing to destroy the trust of the other.
3. Ensure that there is full, free, open and honest communication about anything and everything, internal or external, which has a bearing on the success or failure of the relationship.
4. Be flexible and able to adapt to changed circumstances.
5. Be considerate of each other's rights and feelings and try not to do things to hurt the other in any way.
6. Understand the nature of personal power, and act accordingly.

Let us discuss these six areas in some detail.

Co-operation

For most people, adopting a co-operative manner of living involves enormous changes. First, we have to rid ourselves of our self-centred view of life. Most of us who have this problem — and it is very widespread — don't even recognise it as a problem that we have. For example, one of us has a close acquaintance named Harriet. When we try to have a conversation with her, she listens only to enough of what we say so that she can switch the conversation back to herself. She really shows no interest at all in what is being said, so a dialogue with her might go like this:

Self: You remember Bill? He and his wife dropped in unexpectedly last week. Their new Mercedes was stolen from their driveway recently, and both he and Eileen were quite upset about it.

Harriet: I know what it's like. I had a Range Rover stolen in similar circumstances. I parked it outside our shop for ten minutes. When I came out it was gone. You have no idea of the trouble I had getting the insurance company to pay up.

Self: Bill was really upset. They'd saved up for years to buy the Merc. Apparently the police weren't optimistic about finding the car.

Harriet: I'm still angry about the whole affair. I reported it to the police immediately, but they were useless. The vehicle has never been seen since.

Harriet's conversation shows that she has no interest at all in Bill's problems or for how Bill or his wife might feel. Everything that is said is immediately made self-referent and becomes a launching pad for talking about herself and her own feelings.

The same self-centred approach can be seen in a conversation between a husband and wife.

Wife: I'm really worn out. My car wouldn't start this morning and I had to call the automobile club. They took an hour to arrive. Then I had to buy a new battery and I've been running late all day. I had to cancel my 9 a.m. appointment at the dentist altogether. Then I had to chair a meeting at the school and the others weren't very happy when I arrived late and some of them made some very nasty cracks about being irresponsible.

Husband: You think you've had a bad day! My secretary was away with the flu, and I had this important meeting with the managing director of Zircon Industries. The documents for the meeting weren't finished on time and our production manager got an urgent call and had to leave in the middle of the meeting. The whole thing was a shambles. Why do things like that always happen to me?

This parallel, self-centred speech is in no sense co-operative. Where we allow 'I', 'me', 'my', and 'mine' to dominate our thoughts and our conversation, it is very unlikely that we will ever learn to relate to others in a co-operative way. The message we send to the other person is that we are not really interested in their well-being or how they feel or in what they are saying.

In our earlier analysis of power, we found that hostile, angry and aggressive people are self-centred, want their own way and want to dominate and control others. Even though it was less obvious, we saw that fearful, anxious and submissive men and women are also self-centred. Their lives are dominated by self-centred thoughts like 'I might fail', 'He mightn't like me' or 'She might think I'm an idiot if I say that'. Once again, their lives are dominated by 'I', 'me', 'my', and 'mine' and by indecisiveness and perfectionism in their vain attempts to avoid displeasure and disapproval from others.

Co-operation with others clearly involves changing our view of life. We cannot afford hostile, angry and aggressive ways or the attitudes that underlie all of this. Neither can we afford the people-pleasing, peace-at-any-price approach of the anxious ones. Both are self-centred. We need to adopt the solution-centred approach of the assertive ones where we keep cool, where we are prepared to listen carefully to what others say and to respond to them in a way that shows that we are interested in what they have said and in how they feel about it. Hijacking the conversation by immediately talking about ourselves and our experiences is not the way to go if we want to be co-operative.

Co-operation with others also involves recognising that others might have attitudes, ideas and opinions that are different from ours, and that these others have a right to be different. If we think they are wrong, we might try to convince them of this. Similarly, whenever we express an opinion, we might be wrong. Being assertive means listening to others and being flexible enough to change if the others can demonstrate that we were in error. So co-operation involves a readiness to accept that we have made a mistake and a readiness to openly admit that we were wrong.

Insecure men and women tend to get angry, to be inflexible and very unwilling to admit a mistake. They see this admission as a weakness rather than the strength that it really is. Our theory of power states that we are all imperfect, limited and fallible, so we need a way of living that enables us to cope with our mistakes and with our limitations. Both aggressive and submissive people find asking for help wellnigh impossible. Assertive men and women accept their limitations and find that asking for help is easy and involve others in a co-operative way.

It is hard to see how any close relationship can survive and grow if either partner is not co-operative. It matters little whether the partnership is in business, friendship, or one involving love and affection. Co-operative behaviour is essential for the success of all relationships.

Above all else, co-operation will not survive for long where one or both partners displays anger, hostility and aggressive behaviour towards the other. How can we expect a partner to put up with a constant stream of criticism, with being put down and belittled, with an unrelenting stream of sarcasm or with suspicion and jealousy? How can it be maintained where intolerance and impatience are the order of the day? How can we expect our partners to put up with us when we subject them to a reign of fear resulting from our demanding, threatening, punishing and vengeful behaviour? How must they feel when we constantly interrupt them and even finish their sentences for them? How can co-operation flourish where one partner wants to be top dog, to win and get his or her own way all the time?

How can we expect co-operative behaviour to flourish where we go around walking on eggshells, full of anxiety that we will lose the love or respect of our partner? How can the anxious ones ever have a satisfactory relationship when they feel it necessary to weigh carefully every word they say and give their power away in an incessant desire to keep the peace at any price? How can any relationship flourish where communication is self-censored because of anxiety?

Co-operative behaviour depends on both partners being secure enough to speak openly about their feelings and on feeling safe enough to express these emotions. We all have the power to act in a co-operative way and to encourage our partners to be equally assertive, helpful, thoughtful and considerate. At first, many of us will find change risky. Take a chance. The rewards of using our power in these co-operative ways can be enormous.

Trust

There is a tendency in our community to link the breakdown of trust in a relationship to indulgence in sexual affairs outside that relationship. While it is true that there is probably no quicker and surer way of destroying trust than this, there are also other destructive ways of behaving that bring the same result. Because assertive men and women respect the rights and feelings of their partners, because they are internally directed and not dependent on external sources for praise and affirmation of their worth, they are unlikely to indulge in sexual relationships outside their close primary one. They also have no time for lies and secrecy. Additionally, they tend to see the keeping of promises as very important in their lives and they tend to be consistent in their behaviour. Overall, their partners see them as dependable and have little or no trouble placing their trust in them, so let's look at these factors that are related to the growth and maintenance of trust in a relationship, beginning with honesty and openness.

Honesty and openness Telling lies has been described as a 'prostitution of the mind'. Anxiety-ridden individuals frequently keep the truth from their partners, hoping to avoid criticism. For example, an anxious woman who does not work outside the home may respond to her husband's query about what she has been doing during the day by saying 'Oh, nothing very exciting. I just cleaned up after last night's party and pottered about'. In reality, some weeks previously she had decided to go back to work and had spent much of each day attending job interviews. Terrified of her husband's reaction, she has continually put off telling him about this. Almost inevitably, he is going to find out and, irrespective of his attitude to his wife's working, may be furious or sad and disappointed that she had not trusted him enough to discuss the issue with him.

The assertive way of handling this situation would have been to discuss the position with him from the beginning. This does not mean that she should have dropped the idea of returning to full employment if he had disagreed, but rather that it would have been preferable to tell him of her decision and of the reasons for that decision, listening to his reply and carefully considering his response. If he objected on grounds she considered inadequate, it might be sensible to point out the benefits, which might be about her lack of feelings of well-being, about her boredom, as well as about the financial benefits that might result. Handled calmly and firmly, her husband might well agree, even if reluctantly. She has a right to seek employment unless the reasons not to do so are compelling, and that situation is very rare.

Angry, hostile and aggressive people tell lies to gain an advantage, to maintain control, to come out on top and get their own way. Thus, the husband of this woman may have agreed to ask one of his golfing partners who owns a large firm if there were any job vacancies that might suit his wife. He does this, hoping that the answer will be no. In fact there is a suitable position. When his wife asks whether he has spoken to his friend, he tells her that no suitable jobs were available. This is a lie designed to ensure that she doesn't get a job. He wants to control and dominate her and to get his own way, perhaps because the idea of his wife's getting a job, becoming financially independent and meeting other people, is a threat to him. If she were to find out that he had lied to her, this might result in a furious row or even worse. Lies rarely pay off in the long run. It is far better to trust your partner to do sensible things and not to do anything to harm the relationship.

This man's lie was self-centred and dishonest, and part of being assertive is being open and honest with others. Another part of being assertive is to change from focusing on the self to focusing on finding a solution to the problem. The problem the husband was centred on was finding a way of preventing his wife from getting a job because of his selfish, self-centred desire to prevent her from working. The real problem, which he totally ignored, included her feelings of boredom, worthlessness and discontent with her lifestyle.

Sometimes the dishonest behaviour arises out of a desire to 'protect' the partner from unpleasant news and events. For example, one partner may receive a request to come to the school to discuss a problem that has arisen. On arrival, he or she finds that their eldest child has been absenting himself from school quite frequently. Not wanting to upset the partner, who has just been promoted, this information is withheld and attempts are made to fix the problem alone.

Months later, the problem worsens when the child is suspended from school because he has been using marijuana in the school basement and is suspected of selling it to others. Of course, this can't be covered up, and the working partner gets angry because he or she was not consulted earlier and is not happy with the explanation: 'You were so busy, and I didn't want to upset you'.

An assertive person would have involved the other partner from the beginning, so that together they could have tried to discover why the truanting behaviour was taking place. Both parties have a right to know about everything that has or may have an effect upon their relationship. We have to trust our partner, who is strong enough to handle bad news, and truanting from school is almost always a sign of a quite severe problem.

So being secretive, which goes hand-in-hand with telling lies, also destroys trust in relationships. Those of us who use our power constructively try to be open with our partner, not closed up and secretive. We do not try to protect our partner by withholding information that we judge to be unwelcome. We respect our partner's strength and the right to know, and we give honest information about everything of importance.

Keeping promises The second element in the maintenance of trust is the keeping of promises. There are at least two ways in which promises are seen to be broken. These correspond with the notion of sins of omission and sins of commission. For example, if a wife says she will be home from a function before midnight and does not arrive until two in the morning, this is the equivalent of a sin of commission. If her husband promises to fix a broken light switch at the weekend and doesn't do so, this also falls into the sins of commission category. These activities may be of greater or lesser importance, but any sin of commission like these will lead to some degree of breakdown in trust.

Sins of omission include avoiding responsibility for playing our part in the relationship. Frequently this comes about when one partner becomes so immersed in an occupation and with making money that he or she is just not around for a graduation or a school play in which a son or daughter is acting, or to help with some health crisis such as the removal of an appendix, or the birth of a child. These sins of omission can have quite profound and lasting effects, including the undermining of trust.

They usually mean that someone has their priorities out of kilter, seeing relationships as less important than meetings, than getting involved in a drinking session or, more usually, making money.

Obviously we should try to keep all our promises so, like assertive people, we should be very careful about making them. Don't make a promise unless there is a strong possibility you can keep it. Of course, we sometimes make promises we can't keep. For example, if we promise to pick someone up at a certain time, our car breaks down and there is no way to contact the other person, all we can do is to explain later why we failed to turn up.

Being consistent Another factor that seems to play an important role in the growth and maintenance of trust is displaying a fair degree of consistency in our behaviour. For example, it is difficult to relate well to someone whose moods swing wildly over relatively short periods of time. At one moment they are kind, co-operative and supportive. Within minutes and without any apparent reason they might fly off the handle, dig in their toes and become unkind, unco-operative and hostile or sullen, morose and withdrawn. As we now know, these are all states of anger that make it difficult, if not impossible, to relate to them because they push us away.

Similarly, a partner who has a pervasive problem with anxiety is also likely to have a tendency to vacillation and indecision, changing their position to avoid becoming the object of criticism.

If we want others to trust us, it seems that we need to be quite consistent in the way we behave towards them. This is not to recommend that we become rigid, stubborn or inflexible. Of course we need to change our minds or our behaviour if there is clear evidence that we have made a mistake: where we were wrong or where our behaviour was hurtful or likely to lead to harm. We all need this flexibility. It is our habit of being moody or indecisive that we need to work on if we want others to trust us. We should start to worry when someone who knows us well says 'I never know where I stand with you'.

Assertive people tend to be calm, laid-back and relaxed, even when things aren't going well, when they have made a mistake, or even when they are being heavily criticised. They just deal with these problems when they arise even though those around them are angry or in a state of panic. Because they are intent on finding solutions to these situations, they are decisive and are seen by others to be decisive. As they think through their problems carefully before taking action, they tend to succeed more often than not and thus don't have to change their position very often. Others don't see them as moody or inconsistent in their behaviour and thus find it easy to trust them.

Emotional maturity in relationships The most significant factor in destroying trust in close relationships is undoubtedly the emotional immaturity of one or both partners. This immaturity, which is usually accompanied by low self-esteem, low feelings of self-worth and high levels of insecurity, manifests itself in various forms of hostility, anger and aggression on the one hand or anxiety and submissiveness on the other. These factors, in turn, result in the abuse or misuse of our personal power, leading to a breakdown in communication and to a lowering of trust, and often to the destruction of the relationship because, somewhere in the process, many of these immature ones seek refuge and an affirmation of their attractiveness in another sexual partner outside the relationship. When this is discovered by the other partner, trust can be completely destroyed.

When an assertive individual has a close relationship with another assertive person the rates of relationship problems of this nature are much lower as these people do not seem to form sexual relationships outside the partnership. One of the major characteristics of assertive men and women is that they are *emotionally independent*. This means that they do not need constant praise and reward from outside sources to feel good about themselves. They are secure, and get their rewards internally just by knowing they have done the best they can. Of course, we all like external rewards; we all thrive on praise; we purr when someone tells us we have done well. The difference between the assertive men and women and those who are aggressive or submissive is that when we become assertive, we *want* but don't *need* praise from others. Needing praise is a childlike state that leaves us very vulnerable to lack of praise and especially to criticism.

Assertive men and women have learned how to live comfortably without external sources of praise and to handle the various forms of criticism without losing their cool. Because they communicate well, and are solution-centred rather than self-centred, they tend to fix problems in their relationships and thus are unlikely to have occasion to seek out other sexual partners. By changing ourselves and by changing our perception of ourselves, we become more trustworthy and more trusting in the sexual area.

Avoiding addictions Human beings become addicted to a wide variety of things and activities. The main ones are alcohol, drugs, gambling, tobacco, under-eating and over-eating and work. However, some become addicted to sex, to marathon running, beekeeping, stamp-collecting, rock climbing, dominating others, seeking sensation and avoiding other people. A quick way of telling whether you are addicted is to ask yourself if there is any aspect of your life that takes up most of your time, energy and thoughts to the exclusion of almost anything else.

For example, those who are unfortunate enough to become addicted to alcohol spend a large proportion of their lives drinking alcohol, buying alcohol, thinking about drinking, ensuring that their supplies don't run out, telling others lies about their consumption, hiding their supplies and getting medical treatment for the numerous alcohol-related problems from which they suffer. It is hell being an alcoholic but it is also hell for those close to them who have to put up with their bizarre behaviour, their massive mood swings, their lies and their broken promises. This almost total absorption with alcohol and alcohol-related activities quickly destroys the trust in those close to them. The divorce and separation rates in relationships where heavy drinking and alcoholism are present are astronomically high, partly because aggressive behaviour is the norm, especially as the disease progresses. Altogether, relationships where addiction to alcohol is present are likely to end in disaster because of a complete breakdown in trust.

The only good thing about alcoholism is that it can be fixed and put into remission by total abstinence from all alcohol. A major part of the treatment for this disease is teaching these men and women how to use their power constructively by becoming assertive, and by ceasing to abuse and misuse the rights of their partners and their families. When this is done properly, these people often go on to lead productive lives and to form trusting, loving, kind and rewarding relationships.

A second addiction that has the same or similar effects on relationships is drug abuse. Surprisingly, to many people, it is the legal drugs often prescribed by medical practitioners that cause far more problems than do the illegal drugs. It is the tranquillisers, pain-killers and drugs to help you sleep that are the most dangerous.

Why is it that such a large number of us use alcohol and these drugs at all? The major reason seems to be that we have emotional problems, especially with surges of crippling anxiety that make it difficult for us to speak in public or even to go to a social function. Alcohol and tranquillising drugs make us feel better by slowing down the action of our nervous system and temporarily making us feel more confident. Unfortunately, they have addictive properties that destroy our lives and the trust of those around us.

Clearly, we need another solution that does not involve these drugs. We have shown that it is possible to change these destructive emotional states of anger and anxiety and to learn to become calm and assertive. These mind- and mood-altering drugs don't work in the long run and can wreck our lives. Only by getting to like ourselves, only by concentrating on finding solutions to our day-to-day problems, only by taking control of our lives and becoming firm and decisive can we hope to have serene and happy lives, where those who are near and dear to us can invest their trust in us.

We hear a lot about the destructive nature of heroin, cocaine, amphetamines and other illegal drugs. All we hear about the disastrous effects of these drugs is true, but when we look at the small number of people affected by them when compared with the huge number addicted to alcohol and tranquillisers, the question of addiction takes on a truer perspective.

Of the other addictions, gambling destroys trust most rapidly. The effects include many of those associated with alcoholism. Gamblers usually tell lies to cover up their activities; their whole life centres on making a big killing. Without telling their partners, they embezzle money, often mortgage their homes or secretly borrow huge sums of money to pay their debts. As with alcoholism, suicide often seems to be the only way out, and inevitably families suffer as trust and relationships break down.

The so-called minor addictions aren't really minor at all. Addiction to work and to making money, for example, is one of the worst of these 'minor' addictions because it entails neglect of our most important relationships, which must suffer when the home becomes just a place to eat and sleep before going back to the workplace.

All in all, any addiction is almost certain to place a close relationship in jeopardy, because the focus is on the wrong area. It is our close relationships that can bring us happiness, and these relationships are the ones we need to think about and to focus on. Only by avoiding addictions and addictive behaviour can we keep the trust that is so essential for good relationships and for long-term serenity and well-being.

Assertive people, by definition, don't have major problems with anger and anxiety or allow themselves to become addicted. They are solution-centred, not self-centred, and intent on communicating clearly with those close to them, so they are unlikely to get involved with addictions of any sort or description.

Communication

Improving our communication with our partners, our children and our friends, as well as with those with whom we interact at work and in our sporting and social lives, is a major part of being assertive. Obviously, all the areas we have already covered in this book are related to the effectiveness of our communication. In general, breakdown in communication will result from:

(a) any form of anger, hostility or aggression based on the need to dominate and to control others, or
(b) any form of fear or anxiety based on the need to keep the peace at any price or the need to avoid criticism.

More particularly, breakdown will occur when either partner behaves in ways that are unco-operative and lead to the breakdown of trust, or when they become addicted to alcohol, drugs, gambling, over- or under-eating, or fall victim to any of the minor addictions. Under these headings we discussed secrecy and telling lies, breaking promises, self-centred behaviour, failure to respect the rights and feelings of others, refusal to accept our own limitations, inability to ask for help, 'protection' of our partners, inconsistency in our behaviour, sexual affairs outside the relationship and emotional dependence in seeking praise and reassurance from others.

Given that we concentrate on improving our communication by working hard on all these aspects of our lives, there are still further ways of improving our assertiveness skills.

The big breakdown in communication comes about because there are two areas of our lives that need to be talked about and brought into the open. The first area is the facts, the things that are happening, the problems we face. The second area is how we feel about these facts, these happenings and these problems. Many of us are quite happy to communicate about the facts, but find it very difficult to talk about our feelings in relation to these facts.

What we have seen in our analysis of power is that it is our emotional problems with anxiety and the various forms of anger that lead to major breakdowns in communication and in our relationships. Not only do we have to work hard to lower our states of anger and anxiety but we also have to learn to discuss them with others.

A big problem in our society is that some of us are taught that emotional states should be hidden and kept secret, whereas the best thing to do is to accept them as an important part of living and to talk about them. To deny them and to bottle them up is dangerous, so if someone has accused you falsely of stealing and you feel angry, the idea is to calm down and say 'You're wrong, and I felt very angry about what you just said. The facts are that those materials were sent to our other plant because they had an unexpected shortage. Here's the documentation. I don't like being falsely accused of stealing. In future, I think it would be a good idea if you check your facts before you fly off the handle like that'.

How can we get to work on managing the various forms of anger and lowering our anxiety unless we get in touch with our emotions? In the past, we have probably been taught a lot of nonsense about feelings. How absurd it is to be taught that 'grown men don't cry' or 'all men must be strong and brave'. It's OK for men to cry if they feel sad and sometimes the sensible thing to do when there is danger is to run.

In close relationships, the partners should be open with each other and be prepared to talk about anything, including their feelings. One of the saddest things in life is that, in general, the closer our relationship with someone, the harder we find it to communicate. Thus the communication between many partners is at the lowest level of all. The reasons for this probably include the fact that the more important things are, the greater the consequences of failure. So we might be terrified that our partner will cease to love us if we are open and honest, and we clam up and say nothing.

The best communication occurs where both partners are open, honest, tolerant and direct. Of course we have to respect rights and feelings and do nothing to deliberately harm the other, but in the end we have to work out the most sensible thing to say and say it.

Aggressive and non-assertive behaviours are not concerned with clear communication and with consideration for the rights of the other person, whereas assertive behaviour is. An example will clarify this difference. A young male has decided to pluck up courage and tell his mother he is going to marry a woman he has known for many years. As a first step, he wants to invite her home for a meal with the aim of introducing her to his mother. In the past, his mother has always dominated him: she chose the school he went to, decided that he should become a mechanic and, in fact, has played a major role in every big decision in his life. He now realises that trying to please her has become the main motive in his life and that he needs to change. He has practised being assertive at work and with his friends and found that it paid off. In deciding what to say to his mother, he considered three options, one assertive, one aggressive and one in his customary submissive role.

Assertive option 'Mother, I have some good news. I've been going out with a lovely woman called Jean and I am going to marry her. I want to invite her home for dinner so that she can meet you. I have arranged for her to come next Saturday at seven. I assume that will be OK with you.'

Aggressive option 'In the past you have never allowed me to do anything without asking you first. I'm sick to death of that and the way you carry on about everything. Whether you like her or not, I'm getting married to Jean. She's coming to dinner next Saturday. If you're not nice to her, we will walk out, and I won't be back.'

Non-assertive option 'I've met this woman called Jean, and I was wondering if it would be OK if I invited her home some time soon. I hope you like her, because I'm thinking of marrying her. What do you think?'

The definition of the problem to be solved might be: 'I want to inform my mother that I have met a woman I intend to marry and that I want to bring her home for dinner. What's the best way to do that?'

Quite clearly, the non-assertive option will not solve the problem because it does not specify how he feels about Jean, nor does it specify when he wants to bring her home, or why he wants to do this. It leaves the domineering mother with many easy ways to refuse or delay. For example, she might respond: 'Yes, that's nice. We will have her over some time soon' or 'Well, I'm pretty busy, but I'll see what can be arranged' or 'I think you're too young to be getting married just yet. Wait until you are making more money'.

The aggressive option contains at least four remarks that are likely to make the mother angry, and are almost certain to make her resent and dislike Jean without even meeting her. Even if she did agree to the dinner, it would almost certainly be an uncomfortable meal for everyone. His aggressive, angry tone gives his mother the chance to change the subject completely by accusing her son of not respecting her rights because she is being told quite rudely what will happen if she refuses to co-operate. This is the very form of emotional blackmail that the son resents in his mother.

The final remark in the aggressive approach was: 'If you're not nice to her, we will walk out, and I won't be back'. This is a non-negotiable demand, not an assertive remark like 'I assume that will be OK with you', which does leave open an option for the mother to state that she would prefer the following week, but really puts her on the spot if she wants to say 'no'. The non-assertive option finished with 'What do you think?', a question that left the situation open to any sort of manipulation by the domineering mother.

The second part of asserting ourselves is to realise that if we insist on protecting our own rights and feelings, *we must grant others the right to protect their rights and feelings* unless they behave in ways that make them impossible to communicate with. In the above example, the mother certainly has the right to be consulted about someone being asked for dinner, and the right to be informed about someone her son intends to marry. If she refuses to meet the woman or is discourteous to her when she comes, these rights would vanish and the son would be faced with a new problem about the best way to act from that point on. An assertive response might be to take the mother aside and say 'I understand your reaction about Jean because you are a very possessive woman. However, I want you to stop being rude and start being courteous to her. She has a right to be made welcome here. She really is a nice person and you would like her if only you would give her a chance. I do not have to tolerate rudeness. I *am* going to marry her and I would like to remain on friendly terms with you but that will be difficult unless you accept the decision and be pleasant to her'.

This statement begins by showing that he can understand his mother's feelings and actions. However, it immediately goes on to describe her behaviour as *discourteous* and asks for an immediate change. The statement becomes even more assertive at the end, with a calm comment that if she continues, their relationship may be endangered.

The assertive option contains many of the elements that are necessary for the constructive use of our power.

(i) There is a clear and concise description of the issue. All the main *facts* are presented.

(ii) The son's *feelings* are described in a few words: (a) the news is good, and (b) he likes Jean so much that he intends to marry her.

(iii) He is protecting his own rights and feelings by telling his mother about his intentions.

(iv) He has been open, honest and direct with his mother. The news has been presented calmly but firmly. It is clear that he is not asking for permission to marry Jean, and that he will indeed marry her even if his mother is opposed to the idea. That is, his old habits of being dependent on his mother for approval are no longer a factor.

(v) Furthermore, he has been considerate of his mother's rights by informing her of his plans and of his assumption that the invitation for the following Saturday will be OK with her. All in all, he is firmly taking control of his own life and inviting his mother to co-operate.

Let's turn now and examine ways of expressing our negative feelings. An assertive way of doing this is to objectively describe what is upsetting us, describe how this is affecting our life, describe our feelings about this, and calmly outline what we want to happen.

In a domestic setting where one partner has rejected an invitation to go out to dinner at the home of some mutual friends without consulting the other, the response might be:

Assertive option 'I've just found out we were invited to dinner by Bill and Caitlin. It seems that you refused the invitation without consulting me. I like them, and I enjoy their company. When I heard about it, I felt quite angry, and I'm feeling lonely because we hardly ever go out together these days. This isolation from others is making me feel depressed. In future, I want you to consult me about these matters, and I want you to reconsider the importance of mixing with other people.'

Aggressive option Sulk for two days and speak to your partner only in monosyllables. Eventually when challenged about your moodiness, you say 'I'm really fed up with you. How dare you refuse to go to Bill and Caitlin's without asking me if I wanted to go'.

Submissive option Say and do nothing. Even though you might feel hurt, you find some excuse to keep quiet and say to yourself 'If I say anything, he'll get angry, and I couldn't stand that. Anyway, he's been very busy re-organising his department at work. I suppose he just forgot to ask me about the dinner party'.

This submissive way of handling the issue is based on the need to keep the peace at any price and amounts to condoning the partner's behaviour, so she or he is more likely to do it again whenever it suits. It fails to protect one partner's rights, and communication about that person's wants and needs is zero. Finding excuses for the other's self-centred behaviour avoids the issue altogether.

The aggressive option is based on sulking, on totally withholding communication about the issue for days, and, in what is presumably an attempt to punish, leaving the other in the dark about her or his feelings; perhaps feeling guilty is also involved. The main objectives of the enterprise are to point out that such behaviour is unacceptable and to express a desire for change in the future. These objectives are obviously not going to be achieved by using this option.

The assertive option covers the four points listed above, leaves the other in no doubt about what the issue is, how she or he feels about it, and what is required in the future.

Sometimes we may wish to tone down our assertive remarks in close relationships. We can do this by beginning with a statement that softens our approach, but is followed by the same assertive remarks. Often this empathic beginning gets the other's attention in a positive way. So in the above example, the partner might begin with: 'I realise that you have been under a great deal of pressure at work lately, but I've just found out ...' or 'I can understand why you acted the way you did, but I've just found out ...'

Communication also depends to some degree on our capacity for being flexible in our relationships with others as opposed to being stubborn, rigid and inflexible.

Being Flexible

One of the major hindrances to good communication is where one or both partners starts with an idea, a position, an opinion or an attitude about a particular problem or issue and is prepared to stick to and defend that point of view to the end. No matter what convincing arguments their partner puts up, they refuse to change, but dig in their toes and refuse to admit that they may be wrong or that their partner has a better appreciation of the situation or a better solution to the problem. They are stubborn, pig-headed, arrogant and inflexible, so communication with them about the issue is virtually impossible. Those of us who are like this tend to be hostile, angry and aggressive towards others who have different ideas, values, beliefs and attitudes, to be intolerant and impatient and to abuse our power.

On the other hand, some of us change our opinions as soon as it becomes clear that our partner disagrees with us. We abandon our ideas at the first sign of opposition. We give in. This is, of course, carrying flexibility to extremes and those around us soon come to regard us as weak, vacillating, indecisive and 'never sticking to our guns'. Those of us who are like this tend to be anxious and fearful.

To use our power constructively, we need to learn to listen carefully to what those around us have to say and to consider what they have said very thoroughly. We need to remember that we are all imperfect, limited in our knowledge and basically flawed, so it is always possible that we are mistaken in our views and may need to modify our original ideas, to change our position or even to abandon our original stance completely.

On the other hand, if we are not convinced that the other person has anything constructive to add to the debate and if we are still convinced that we have got it right, we need to be strong enough to defend what we have said and try to convince the other to change. The flexibility in this case lies in being prepared to listen and to think about the argument being put up.

One of the big problems in being flexible is that, even though the world around us is changing rapidly, most of us have formed attitudes and beliefs very early in our lives and refuse to examine them to see if they are still valid, decades later. This is not to advocate abandoning our principles lightly. For example, we may have acquired an attitude in our childhood that it is essential to be honest in our dealings with others. It seems unlikely that we will ever need to change that attitude.

Given the very rapid pace of change, however, continual reassessment of the ways in which we behave and of our attitudes and beliefs seems to be essential. This is part of our growth. We cannot afford to become self-satisfied and complacent in a society which is in such a state of flux. In one sense, we never reach a perfect state of maturity, so we need to remain flexible.

Being Considerate of Others' Rights and Feelings

Earlier in the book we looked at some of the basic rights that we need to protect if we are to take charge of our own lives. In that discussion, it was made clear that our partners, and all of those with whom we come into contact, share these same rights and feelings and that it is essential that we do not deliberately trample on their rights or do anything to hurt their feelings.

It appears that being inconsiderate and thoughtless is based on our self-centred, centre-of-the-universe theory of life where we give little or no thought to our partner's rights and feelings. How can we possibly form lasting and rewarding relationships when everything we do is centred on 'I', 'me', 'my', and 'mine' and when 'you', your', and 'yours' get a mention only when someone has to be blamed, put down by sarcastic remarks, or abused or punished?

One right we all share is to make mistakes now and then. This right is necessary because of our inborn limitation and fallibility. One of the important consequences of this is that we not only need to learn to forgive ourselves when we make a mess of things, say things we later regret or do things that are far from sensible, but we also need to learn to forgive others when they display their imperfection in these selfsame ways.

The problem is that when those of us who are inconsiderate make a mess of things, we tend to try to hide the mistake, cover it up or shift the blame on to someone else. This is a totally unnecessary abuse of our power. When we are found out, as often happens, those around us get angry and treat us with scorn and derision. If we confidently and openly admit our mistakes and accept the occasional blunder as an inevitable part of living, paradoxically those around us tend to admire us for our strength and courage.

When we go out of our way to respect the rights of those around us, they are more likely to respect us and to be more considerate of our rights and feelings.

As anger, hostility and aggressiveness on the one hand, and anxiety, fear and submissiveness on the other, are based on self-centredness, those of us who have these problems are likely to be inconsiderate in our dealings with our partners, and others with whom we come into contact. So the best way to become more considerate is to work on our self-centredness and on these emotional problems that impinge on and influence the way we behave towards others.

Understanding the Nature of Power

One of the major problems with the use of power in marriage and other close relationships is that many of us mistakenly believe that being married to someone gives us special rights to trample on our partner's rights and feelings. When we get married or form a close relationship, we do not acquire *any* special rights, but rather extra responsibilities to be kind, gentle and considerate, and to try to co-operate with our partner for our common good.

The other thing that arises from an understanding of the nature of power is that our partner will not be perfect, and neither will we. The notion of limitation makes this clear. Not only are we limited, fallible and mistake-prone, but so are our partners. Once we begin to change, we are more likely to accept our own imperfection, but may continue to demand perfection from our partner.

One of the main problems in relationships is continuing to misuse or abuse our power. If you are in any doubt at all about the way that any form of hostility, of anger or of aggression will harm your relationship, ask yourself questions such as these:

(i) How do I feel when others approach me in a hostile manner?

(ii) Do I like being on the receiving end of anger and aggression?

We believe that the answer will be 'no' to each question. Not only do we dislike this sort of behaviour but we begin to dislike the one who is angry and aggressive towards us, and good relations with them become impossible.

In the same sort of way, we become distanced from those who are so anxious that they can't be trusted to tell us the truth about their feelings and who are vacillating, dependent, and indecisive.

We just can't have good relationships with those around us

who abuse or misuse their power. They cannot have good relationships with us if we abuse or misuse our power in our dealings with them.

Where both partners are open, honest and direct, where both accept their limitations, where the main motive becomes one of trying to communicate, to make good decisions and to put these decisions into practice, trust can flourish, communication will improve and we can become more considerate of each other's rights and feelings while at the same time protecting our own.

In such an atmosphere, love and affection can survive and grow. Some of us who have been very fortunate have long term-relationships where love and affection is still present after decades of living together, even though it may not be marked by the passion and intensity of the early years. It may have changed to a more mature form, but it is as steady as a rock because trust has grown, because the communication has improved and consideration for the rights and feelings of each other has become a central aim. Above all, both partners have come to accept total responsibility for everything they say, do and feel.

The great bulk of this chapter has been about partnership factors in close relationships. We have concentrated on these areas because of our conviction that these are the ones that are often neglected, leading to their breakdown.

Let's turn now briefly to the final facet that distinguishes marriages and other close relationships from friendships and partnerships of, say, a business kind.

Love and Affection

Marriage and similar close partnerships are very special relationships because of the initial intention of having them last a lifetime and because of the intensity of the emotional involvement and response to each other. We call this intense response *love*, and it is the presence of love and affection that puts marriages and these other close relationships in such a special category.

The word 'love' itself defies definition. Certainly those in love take a passionate delight in being with, in touching and having sex with the other. They often feel bereft when they are out of contact. They delight in being with and doing things with each other. They hold each other dear and show mutual affection. Above all, they will do things for the other partner without thought of reward of any sort. Whatever it is, without it there is not a marriage or close relationship.

The relationship between love and the preceding partnership factors is very complex, but when trust goes, when respect for the other's rights and feelings vanishes, and when communication reaches a very low point, love and affection are usually damaged and may even disappear. If this happens, the relationship to all intents and purposes is over, even if the partners continue to live together in the same house.

One of the problems with the word 'love' is that many people confuse it with sex. Now it is usually true that those who love one another have satisfying sex lives because the really enjoyable sex comes out of love. However, some, and especially females, have sex to keep the peace and for many of these people the love has decayed long ago.

The loss of love and affection is one of the major reasons given by women seeking divorce. When faced with this, some men will say 'But I do love you. Only two months ago I bought you a new wall oven and a dishwasher, and what about that holiday in Fiji?' The women just laugh. Love is not something that can be bought. Sex can.

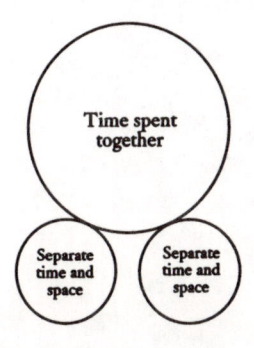

Figure 10.1 Sharing and private space in relationships

Figure 10.1 illustrates that while doing things together and spending a lot of time together are critically important for the success of the relationship, allowance must be made for the fact that each partner needs some private time and space.

The upper oval figure represents the time that the partners spend together doing the garden, walking along the beach, helping one another prepare and cook meals, going to social functions, in recreational, creative and sporting activities and so on. The smaller circles represent the private time and space belonging separately to each partner. This is where they do their own thing because no two people have a total overlap in interests.

This is the sort of thing that tends to happen in good relationships. The partners enjoy being with each other, so this takes up the majority of their time as they help each other and do things together. For the private bits to work, they must trust one another completely to do nothing that will harm the relationship. There is nothing possessive in such relationships, no idea that one owns the other. People cannot own other people. When that idea is present, the relationship is marked by lack of trust and by destructive jealousy. Relationships of this sort rarely work.

chapter 11
Power in Games, Sport and Recreation

We don't have to look very far to see that anger, aggression, and violence of all descriptions are prominent in games and sport. This abuse of power can be found even in non-contact sports like tennis, where the second line of professionals can still earn six-figure annual incomes. Temper tantrums, racquet throwing and verbal abuse of the umpires and linespeople are not uncommon.

In contact sports like all the various codes of football, the rules have been changed and tightened over the years to try to stamp out dangerous and foul play. Yet, in almost every game that is played, the referee or umpire has to stop the game and award penalties against players who persist in attacking an opposite player or who indulge in foul play of one sort or another. Sometimes a particularly bad foul results in an all-in brawl with numbers of players from both teams hurling themselves into the fracas.

Even in organised sport for children at the elementary school level, where one might imagine that the aim is to have fun while practising and learning the skills of catching, passing, throwing, kicking, running and tackling, high levels of aggressive behaviour appear. As soon as it becomes a competition with a prize at the end, parents and relatives with their highly developed attitudes of 'winning is all that matters' begin to appear on the sidelines, hurling abuse at the opposition team, the referee or umpire and encouraging these young children to win at any cost, even if it means deliberately injuring one of the opposition players.

Unfortunately, many of the coaches of these teams condone this violence because they too feel that they are failures if their charges don't win, and they certainly have many, if not all, of the attitudes that underlie hostility, anger and aggression of all sorts.

Somehow, the idea of games and sport as fun and recreation is being lost. Now it is certainly true that games and sports are competitive in nature. Unlike a relationship, the aim for the team or individual playing a game is to emerge as the victor, and when we engage in any game or sport, there is no doubt that to win is desirable. So it is legitimate and sensible to do the best we can to finish up with a better score than our opponent. Competition and being competitive are acceptable.

However, once again, it is our attitude about winning that causes the aggressive problems so pervasive in our society. We are taught and we learn that *we have to win* and when it looks as if we are not going to come out on top, or when we lose, we get angry because even at a very young age we have already learned that to lose, to come second, means that we have failed and indeed that we are failures.

Obviously what we need are new attitudes to both success and failure. Losing and being unsuccessful are an integral part of life as well as sport and games. In the latter, if one individual or team wins, at least one other loses. Do we need to feel despondent, depressed or angry and to go around finding excuses for our failure to succeed or to blame someone else for the loss? Why do this when games can't even begin unless someone is prepared to lose? Our great over-emphasis on the importance of winning is causing massive problems; our attitude towards failure to win is having the same effect.

Success too tends to be over-valued. If we win it is good and we can justifiably feel elated but it doesn't mean that we are superior human beings.

There is another usually overlooked problem involved here, and it surrounds the emotion of anxiety rather than that of anger. The problem is that many of us who suffer from anxiety refuse to play games at all. Somehow or other, we anxious ones recognise the extremely high value that is placed on winning and being the best. Because of the even higher value we place on avoiding criticism and because of our all-pervasive fear of failure, we tend to opt out of competitive games altogether. This is sad, because we cut ourselves off from a significant part of life that is, in many ways, potentially fun and rewarding. We have already seen that the highly anxious tend to avoid promotion at work and find it difficult to mix at social functions. Games and sport form yet another area of living avoided by the anxious.

As in industrial settings, there are many people with potential in the sporting and games area who avoid sport like the plague. It is also true that they avoid playing games like Scrabble and Trivial Pursuit, and card games of all sorts. This avoidance results from the competitive way in which others approach games and because of the anger and aggression generated in so many of their friends and associates when they lose. It is also part of their own fear of losing and of being thought inadequate by the other players.

What then can we do about our own approach to these issues? What can we do about those around us who have problems with games? Let us remember that the only power we have is the power to run our own lives in a sensible way. Let us harness this power so that we can take part in, and enjoy, games as much as possible. We can do something if it is our own anger or anxiety that is causing problems. So let's begin by changing our own behaviour first.

As all games involve some degree of competition and as winning is one of the objectives in all games, we have first to come to terms with these facts. Let's start with competition and being competitive. There is absolutely nothing wrong with being competitive provided it is simply a means of doing the best you can to win the game within the rules. We get into trouble only when we are prepared to break the rules of the game in order to win, when we are prepared to cheat and to lie because *we have to win*, because *we need to win* and where *even the thought of losing is more than we can bear*. When we have attitudes like these, we are likely to get very angry or depressed or to sulk if we don't win.

To counter this, we need to develop new attitudes about games. The first is towards the aims of playing games. We don't have to win. A better attitude might be that games are about enjoying yourself, having fun, and sometimes meeting new people where we do our best to win but where winning is not all-important. The second attitude is about being competitive. We can be highly competitive without becoming angry and aggressive at all. We just do the best we can to win, but don't get upset when the other person or team comes out on top. So we need a new attitude that says: not winning is OK and, as we will lose quite often when we play games, we need to accept our losses with good grace.

Most of us find that being gracious in defeat is quite a difficult process indeed, and we need to practise this skill, which takes a lot of personal courage and strength. When we manage to accept defeat with good grace, our opponent will be delighted and onlookers are likely to think very highly of us. While we don't need the good opinion of the onlookers, all of us feel better when they do think well of us. In a very indirect way, accepting defeat graciously is a way of making friends and ensuring that our popularity rises.

A rise in popularity is what the anxious ones among us seek so desperately. By avoiding games altogether, this avenue of becoming popular is totally cut off. So, the best thing for the anxious to do is to stop over-valuing what others think of them, to take risks and to play as many games as possible without worrying whether they win or lose or whether they are good at the game or not. Those of us who are anxious just have to do the best we can and be satisfied with the outcome, whatever it is.

Dealing with aggressive behaviour from others who play games is something else we need to learn. Above all we have to remember that we are powerless to change these others who behave badly unless they choose to change. But that doesn't mean that we cannot try to persuade them to alter their ways.

Let us imagine that a man becomes very angry when he and his wife lose a game of Scrabble they are playing with visiting friends. Throughout the game he criticises her for her moves, complains about not getting any good letters and bemoans the fact that all the luck seems to be with their opponents. After losing two games, he refuses to play any further, although the other three want to play on.

It would probably be unwise for his wife to say anything to him in front of the visitors but she might speak later in private and say: 'I have a problem I want to discuss with you, and I don't want you to get angry and run away. It's about Scrabble. When we were playing with Mary and David, you got angry because we were not winning, you continually criticised me in front of them and eventually you went off in a huff because we lost two games in a row. I found that aggressive and angry behaviour totally unacceptable. It was ungracious and offensive, and I want you to stop behaving in that way. It's just a game, and it doesn't matter who wins. We will finish up with no friends at all if you continue'.

Now this approach is not guaranteed to make her husband change, but at least it makes him aware that there is a problem, it describes his behaviour as unacceptable, and asks him to change. This is a cool, assertive approach that might work.

Let us consider her other options. Even though she was upset by his behaviour, she could have decided that discretion was the better part of valour and said nothing at all. Almost certainly this would have been seen by him as a licence to continue to behave this way in the future, and the possibility of his changing for the better would be minimal. This is a submissive misuse of power.

A third way would have been to confront him quite aggressively and say 'You really are a pain in the neck. I'll bet Mary and David won't come here again after your childish temper tantrum while we were playing Scrabble'.

This aggressive approach would give her husband an excuse to get angry and to attack her. 'So what! I can't stand that pair anyway. I couldn't care less if I never saw them again. Your

Scrabble playing is abysmal. No one could win playing with you.' Her aggression gave him the opportunity to ignore her remarks about his behaviour and to divert the discussion onto her supposed lack of skill in playing Scrabble.

With someone who is anxious and who refuses to join in a game of cards by saying 'Oh no. I can't play cards very well and I'd spoil it for you', we might try to persuade them to play by saying 'Well, that doesn't matter. It's only a game where we can have fun. It's not important who wins. I'll help you as much as I can'. This is downplaying the seriousness of the outcome, lowering the competitive nature of the game, and it just might succeed in lowering the anxiety level enough for the person to agree to join in.

Perhaps the most difficult area to handle is violence in organised sports like football. What do we do when an opponent kicks us in the shins or gives us a short-arm jab to the face during a tackle? Our instinct, of course, is to retaliate and this is what often happens. The problem with this is that when we do, the original punch might remain unseen and the victim might be penalised for instigating the mêlée. Occasionally, this penalty might even turn the game around and cause the victim's team to lose.

Unfair! It certainly is, but this doesn't help the victim or his team. The most difficult but the most sensible thing to do is to ignore the original attack and hope that the umpire or referee will see it and penalise the real offender. All of these games have rules outlawing such violent and dangerous play and the best we can do is to exercise restraint and trust that the officials will have seen the offence. Even if they don't, adopting the 'eye for an eye' principle is taking the law into our own hands, and society has decided that allowing individuals to become judge, jury and hangman just doesn't work. As a society, we have decided to leave these functions to appointed officials, and the sooner we apply this principle to sport, the better for us all. Fines and periods of suspension for the aggressor might not work at all times, but it is the best system we've got.

In summary, we are suggesting that despite the competitive nature of sport and games, we do not need to abandon our principles. The way of living we have been consistently advocating holds up. We don't need to change our assertive way of living. It will be much more productive if we keep trying to use our power in a constructive way while playing games and sport. Misusing or abusing our power might appear to provide short-term gains, but in the long term they will prove illusory.

chapter 12
The Use of Power in Industrial Settings

Up to this point, we have avoided looking directly at the connection between the way we use our power and the accumulation of wealth, position and lavish lifestyle. However, many in our society equate power with acquiring vast sums of money, with holding high positions in industry or government and with being able to use this wealth and position to influence the lives of their employees or even to influence government decisions about financial policies, taxation policy, foreign affairs policy and especially trade and tariff policy.

These men and women certainly have the ability to influence the lives of thousands, even tens of thousands, of their fellow citizens. Those who own and control the newspapers, television outlets, radio stations, satellites and other media outlets are in a position where their decisions can and do have quite profound effects on those around them. This is the sense in which these people are often described as 'powerful'. We prefer to use the word 'influential' and to reserve the word 'powerful' to describe those who consistently use their power to run their own lives sensibly and constructively, and to improve their quality of life in various ways.

To make this point patently obvious, let's look at the business scene of the 1980s. In this decade we saw the rise of entrepreneurs who rapidly accumulated vast sums of money by using borrowed capital to take over company after company. Many of these entrepreneurs became well known for their lavish lifestyle, for buying the most expensive houses in the most expensive neighbourhoods, acquiring the paintings of world-famous artists, and entertaining in the most luxurious ways. For many, following the 1987 crash on the stock exchanges around the world, the expensive cars, houses and country estates have gone. The works of art have been sold. Some of these high flyers are in prison working out their sentences for fraud, embezzlement and other corporate crimes. Others are still to face the courts or are involved in lengthy and protracted trials on a variety of charges. How can we describe these people as powerful when their lives were dominated by greed in their self-centred abuse of their personal power? For a time, envied by many for their wealth, they certainly were influential. In the long term, however, their continual abuse of their own personal power has brought many of them to their knees.

There were, of course, many other astute businesspeople who weathered the storm and who are now building up their wealth again as the world emerges from recession. Many of these men and women rarely make the headlines in the newspapers, or act in the flamboyant ways described above. They don't seek publicity and above all they rarely have the arrogance displayed by some of their fellows. They use their personal power much more constructively.

To make this point clear, let's look at some business success stories that have been emerging in the press since 1993 showing how businesses in Australia, both large and small, have changed their work practices to cope with the need to move into the export market and to become more efficient and competitive as the internationalisation of trade becomes more and more apparent.

One approach has been the adoption of 'international best practice', which simply means examining work practices to find the best possible way of doing things in industrial settings. Co-operation between the Australian Federal Government and the Australian Manufacturing Council has led to many industrial organisations developing a more competitive workplace culture. In turn, this has resulted in improved productivity, better industrial relations, and greater organisational flexibility. Let's look at two examples from large industries as reported in *Business Review Weekly* in December 1993.

CIG Gas Cylinders, based in Sydney, manufactures aluminium gas cylinders. During 1990, the management of CIG became convinced that productivity could best be improved by 'empowering' their workforce by setting up self-managing work teams.

> These teams were developed through a consultative process with input from management, owners of the company, employees and unions. A comprehensive analysis of work organisation was undertaken by a team of five shopfloor, one trades, one supervisor and two management employees. The team identified problem areas and recommended a redesigned system which was introduced in July, 1991.

With its emphasis on explaining the new concept to everyone concerned, and with the introduction of self-managing work teams, CIG is currently the biggest supplier of aluminium cylinders to Japan, where it has gained an 18 per cent share of the market, a share which the management believes it can increase to 45 per cent by 1995.

The increase in productivity and efficiency brought about by using their power constructively has allowed CIG Gas Cylinders to win a lucrative contract with Coca-Cola in Japan because the company could supply cylinders from Sydney to Japan more quickly than could the local suppliers.

Using similar procedures, Du Pont (Australia) saw their Girraween plant's production of graphic art film per labour hour increase by more than 150 per cent between January 1992 and March 1993. This performance was so dramatic that Du Pont decided to close a film-finishing factory in Japan and service the Japanese market from Australia, adding thirty million dollars to the Australian plant's sales, and creating many new jobs.

As with CIG, both managers and employees at Du Pont underwent training to help them develop the attitudes and skills necessary for change. The manager

> emphasises that the focus of training is on empowering staff to make decisions about their work practices and ways of improving procedures. Leadership and team building skills are being provided through a series of courses which cover a range of topics such as time management, project and task planning, oral presentation, team development, and team effectiveness.

It is not only the larger industries that benefit from the recent emphasis on participative management, and this new-found realisation that the old antagonistic 'us versus them' management style is not viable in the 1990s, where industries need to enlarge their market by becoming export-oriented and necessarily more productive and competitive. It seems that only by a co-operative approach by management and workers can this quantum leap in productivity be gained. The same approach is now seen to be paying off in small businesses of fewer than one hundred employees.

A recent development in the small business field has been the setting up of State and National Small Business Awards. Introducing the winners of the 1993 Awards, the Chairman of the Business Council of Australia Innovation Study Commission Group, Sir Roderick Carnegie, said: '... if companies get management and employees to work together as a team, everything else falls into place'. This co-operative theme was stressed by the overall winner for 1993, Hunter Valley Rewinds, a small electric motor repair and rewind company in New South Wales. The Managing Director said that the reason for the success 'was the attitude of the staff and the comfortable relationship between customers, suppliers and company ... this all comes from a team effort'.

The winner of the Total Quality Award was WGE of Port Kembla. This company started out as a backyard enterprise and now has 150 employees, providing engineering support for heavy industry. It is now in the process of establishing a company in Vietnam and has established links with Kuwait and Japan. A spokesman for the company said 'We are now selling to Japan what they used to sell to us ... we go to any lengths to give the customer what they want ... We look to our staff to achieve their personal goals and then profit will be an automatic thing'.

All the winners stressed the importance of retraining staff and of involving staff and management in a co-operative venture. They speak of the loyalty to the firm that such an approach engenders. It seems that the constructive use of power we have been describing throughout this book is just as important in business and industry as it is in our personal, social and recreational life. The most significant point is that honest, open and friendly communication and co-operative behaviour seem to pay off in business whether it be large or small. It is clear that, in the businesses we have been describing, this co-operative behaviour involves everyone including the Federal Government, trade unions, business organisation, management and workers. Just as close relationships thrive on high levels of communication and co-operation, so do all of those involved in a business or industry run in a co-operative manner. Productivity goes up, profits rise, wages and salaries go up and the workplace becomes a happier and safer environment. Even the government benefits from the higher return of taxation and eventually this flows down to the whole community.

Of course, not every manager and not every firm is moving in this direction. There are many, in fact a majority, who still retain the old rigid hierarchical structures where power is firmly held at the top. There are still those in small businesses who say 'This is my business, I built it up. No one else understands it like I do, and there is no way I'll allow anyone else to tell me how to run my business'. This is the arrogance we have spoken of before. It is self-centred and rests on the assumption of perfection: 'I know it all.' This is not very sensible. No owner or manager is perfect, and there may be men and women in the firm with many worthwhile ideas about how the work practice can be improved and altered but the owner is too arrogant, too rigid to listen. It is interesting to note that a recent analysis of business bankruptcy concluded that the vast majority of bankruptcies in the recent recession were due to poor management and not to the downturn in the business cycle.

This brings us to the area of how we are to conduct ourselves in our occupations. Do we need to believe the creed expressed in the musical *How to Succeed in Business without Really Trying*, or can talented men and women rise to the top while remaining cool, calm and co-operative, using their power constructively? While we have evidence that businesses flourish where a co-operative spirit permeates the whole organisation, we have no such evidence, one way or the other, when it comes down to individual progress within an organisation.

On the other hand, we think it safe to assume that an individual who rises to the top in a large organisation by lying, cheating, spreading false rumours about his or her peers and by sticking daggers in their backs will have little or no chance of inspiring feelings of loyalty or even respect from those who have borne the brunt of such aggressive manipulation. Without this loyalty and respect, it seems unlikely that the organisation will grow and prosper under the direction of such an individual.

Watching successful men and women who appear on television and who command very high salaries, it would seem that the majority belong in the assertive group who use their power constructively. They come across as friendly but firm, strong but not arrogant, assertive but not aggressive. They seem to be good decision-makers and not likely to panic. Probably they are extremely hardworking, so that characteristic is not restricted to those who are aggressive in their dealings with others. They appear to be prepared to listen to views that differ from their own and to be flexible enough to change when the evidence suggests that they are wrong. Overall we believe that, more often than not, the cream will come to the top in large organisations, provided that the promotion criteria depend upon ability and skill and not solely on factors such as length of service or on nepotism. However, because the promotion system is imperfect, there will be enough exceptions to the rule to convince some of us that the whole system is corrupt and that the only hope is to act aggressively, to treat our colleagues as enemies and to plot and connive. This way is likely to fail. It will certainly alienate those around us.

We do not mean to suggest that becoming assertive and using your power constructively will automatically guarantee your success in being promoted, reaching the top or even making lots of money. For one thing, we need ability and skill to achieve these ends. What we do suggest is that if we use our power constructively we are much more likely to achieve a level appropriate to our ability and level of skill and not remain at some level below that.

In Australia, it is not only large and small secondary industries that are profiting from this approach. In March 1993, the Prime Minister announced the nine national winners of a Federal Government's scheme aimed at protecting and enhancing land and water resources throughout the country. By March 1994, almost 2000 Landcare groups were functioning, attempting to turn the tide against land and water degradation.

One of the winners of the Landcare Awards was the Lake Towerinning Catchment Landcare Group in Western Australia, where a whole community bonded together to save a fresh-water lake, which had become two-thirds as salty as sea water. By diverting a creek from twelve kilometres away, they flushed out the salt and returned the lake to such a pristine condition that the community is now thinking about reintroducing freshwater fish.

In another project named Trees For Life, a single landcarer surprised farmers by organising an innovative project in which rural and city people worked together to put millions of trees into the ground on farms, free of cost to the farmers, helping to revegetate South Australia. Altogether 9.25 million trees were raised through the programme, with volunteers as the driving force.

In the New South Wales area around Gosford, just to the north of Sydney, the Gosford City Council won a Landcare Award for implementing a policy that ensured care for the land around Gosford. 'Their code of practice on erosion and sedimentation control means the land comes first. If a road is built in the area, the slopes are progressively replanted to stop the wash-off of soil.' A further award went to the Emerald High School in Queensland, where the students formed their own company to sell off environmentally friendly products that they made, and got the company listed on the Stock Exchange. This was only one of the seventeen Landcare projects organised within the school, making it the biggest junior Landcare group in Queensland.

As Prime Minister Keating said:

> This country's Landcare movement is uniquely Australian ... Volunteers are the driving force. Landcare is based on a sense of partnership and active participation that makes it a wonderful force for progress. (*The Australian*, 30 March 1994)

There is no doubt that the Landcare project provides us with yet another illustration of the benefits that can be derived when government, business, councils, organisations and individuals use their power constructively and work together on enterprises in such a co-operative way.

Overall it is clear that the constructive use of power produces highly beneficial results and that this outcome occurs in both primary and secondary industries. The principles are the same as in the other areas we have previously considered. Co-operation, openness, honesty and concern for the rights and feelings of others, communication and trust are just as important in industry as they are in our personal and social lives. We don't need a new set of rules to succeed in our occupational lives. Being calm and assertive and using our power constructively work just as well in these areas as they do in others.

Of course, making changes of this nature in the workplace is not easy. These changes involve management, unions and workers in quite profound attitudinal shifts in which we move from a combative, adversarial approach, with its underpinning of hostility, anger and aggressive behaviour, to a more co-operative, friendly and tolerant approach. It becomes necessary for every member of the team to learn to respect the rights and feelings of those around them, irrespective of their place or status in the group. The organisational structure has to be such that it leads to a reduction in stress throughout the firm to such a degree that anxiety and fear are unlikely to rise to a level where productivity is reduced in any way, where creative ideas are stifled, or where the atmosphere is such that those in the workplace feel belittled or foolish if their ideas are impractical or prove less than cost-efficient.

Let's look a little more closely at these attitudinal changes. One of the major necessary shifts surrounds the nature of authority. It is in the area of attitude to authority that both employers and employees will almost certainly need to make quite significant changes. Let's look at the employees first. Earlier in the book it was suggested that those of us who are dominated by our hostility will have an angry, aggressive approach to life that we will possibly carry with us into the workplace. In this atmosphere, we are likely to resent carrying out orders, to be contemptuous of those in positions of authority irrespective of their level of ability, and to characterise those above us in the hierarchy as stupid and ill-trained for the job they hold. Quite clearly, such an attitude will result in lowered performance, poor relationships with authority figures and perhaps in absenteeism, frequent arguments and even strikes.

The main way of helping ourselves to become happier, more productive and more highly paid employees is to work on lowering our anger and resentment levels in the ways suggested earlier. More specifically, it also necessitates changing our attitudes to authority figures in the workplace, so it may pay us to look at the notion of what is entailed in accepting a job.

When we accept a job offer we are agreeing to a contract that may or may not be spelled out. The contract means that we agree to do a certain job to the best of our ability in return for a specific wage or salary. It also implies that we agree to abide by the rules of the organisation and to carry out any *reasonable* request or order from the management team that lies within the job specification to which we agreed. In return, the management has an obligation not to require us to perform activities that demand skills outside those outlined in the contract or to make unreasonable requests of us. For example, if we were hired as a computer programmer, it would be unreasonable for the managing director to require us to act as chauffeur. Within the boundaries of our contract, we should do our job willingly and cheerfully and in as co-operative a way as possible.

In the participative management schemes we have been describing, all members of the team from the least skilled in the organisation to the managing director are seen as valued employees who work together as a team, where suggestions for better ways of organising and doing things are encouraged and where regular meetings of the various teams are held to develop ways of increasing productivity and making the firm more competitive. When this happens, the firm prospers and wage and salary increases become more likely for everyone, not just for those in the higher echelons of management.

On the other side of the coin, those in management positions will need to change their attitudes to being in positions of authority. The main obstacle to this change is personal arrogance where we see ourselves as superior and better than those in less well-paid positions and come to believe that all of this justifies our telling others how things should be done. This approach is self-centred and overlooks one of the major assumptions about personal power: that not a single one of us is perfect, not one of us can ever have a total and perfect grasp of the best way to run everything in what is usually a very complex organisation and activity. Somewhere in the workforce there will be skilled and creative men and women who can come up with better ways of doing things, with creative ideas for making new products, ways of cutting costs and so on.

One of the main jobs of the modern manager would seem to be to accept his or her own limitations and imperfections and to learn to consult those in the workforce and to encourage ideas from them. Those who hold on to their sense of self-importance, who see themselves as all-wise and all-knowing, who look down upon and denigrate people of lower rank, would seem to be poor managers, limited in vision and usually incapable of gaining loyalty and respect. Rises in productivity and competitiveness to meet benchmarks and international best practice would seem to be beyond their capacity unless they change.

chapter 13
Power Sharing

One of the major thrusts of this book has been the emphasis on a co-operative way of living as a constructive use of our personal power. We have consistently argued that an aggressive and self-centred approach to life with little or no concern for the rights and feelings of others will, in the long term, bring us into conflict with them, although it may seem to offer short-term gains.

Similarly, we have argued that an anxious, submissive way of living, which our examination also proved to be self-centred, is unlikely to bring us any happiness or long-term sense of well-being or achievement. Keeping the peace at any price and avoiding making decisions might avert criticism for a while and give us a short-term feeling of security, but in the long term those around us are likely to regard us with contempt and begin to trample on our rights and feelings.

We have argued that the co-operative way of living, where we take control of our own lives by adopting a firm, assertive and solution-centred approach to co-operating with others, works in close relationships, at work and in games, sport and recreation. Life becomes easy. We learn one set of principles, one set of values, beliefs and attitudes and apply all of these to everything we do.

One of these principles is related to time. We have suggested that the only function of past experiences is to learn from our mistakes and try not to repeat them. More positively, we might learn from our successes, provided that they are not gained by taking advantage of others. The things we need to avoid are feelings of anger or depression about our mistakes, guilt about our actions when they were not designed to harm others, or resentment about the behaviour of those around us. The past is past and can't be relived. What we need to do is to work out what we can do in the present to make our lives and the lives of people around us more satisfying.

The only thing we can do about the future is to plan carefully and to do sensible things here and now so that our future, and the future of those with whom we interact, will be more satisfying, rewarding and fulfilling. The big danger occurs when we allow ourselves to worry about events that have yet to occur, fantasise about possible catastrophes and spend so much time out in the future that we have little or no time to deal calmly and effectively with the present reality. Instead we become anxious and full of foreboding. In the long run, it is inevitable that this will lead us into perfectionism and procrastination, both of which end in chaos.

We have also tried to demonstrate the crucial notion of being powerless. *The only legitimate power we have is the power to run our own lives in a sensible way.* We have no legitimate power to dominate, to control or to manipulate the lives of any other human being and especially of those close to us. Our power is limited. We are limited, fallible, and mistake-prone, and it is absolutely critical that we accept this fact. Once we do, we can accept the mistakes we will inevitably make, the fact that others have a right to point these mistakes out to us, and that those around us are similarly limited in their power.

It is easy to overlook the fact that millions of the men and women still living today were born before the arrival of aeroplanes, television, computers, videos and compact disc players. The world as it is today is a vastly different place from what it was in the early twentieth century. The rate of change has not been restricted to technology. There have been huge advances in medical knowledge and practice, in our eating habits, in the way we move about the world, and in our employment opportunities. The roles of the church and the family have changed. In order to deal effectively with this ever-increasing rate of change, we need a system that will enable us to cope. We do not need to become overwhelmed. We do have the power to change to meet these challenges, and we can change, provided we use our power constructively. We will not succeed in changing if we abuse or misuse that power.

By using our power constructively in these calm, solution-centred and co-operative ways, with the full knowledge that we will make mistakes, and say and do the wrong thing from time to time, we will still be able to cope quite well. We can look forward to better health and happier relationships. Only in these ways will we give ourselves a chance to develop our talents, whether they lie in creative or aesthetic fields, in industry, in politics, in helping others, or in sporting activities. Our power is immense. It is up to each of us to use our own power to its fullest extent.

Who can stop us? Nobody but ourselves, because nobody else has the power. We can use our power to overcome the inevitable obstacles. Our personal power is immense.

appendix 1

Appendix 1 contains:
1. *A Score and Level Record table for your own results*
2. *The Self-Analysis Questionnaire Form X–1*
3. *The Self-Analysis Questionnaire Form X–2*
4. *The Anger Expression Scale (AX)*
5. *Directions for scoring and interpreting your scores on:*

      (i) State-Anger
      (ii) Trait-Anger
      (iii) Anger-Control
      (iv) Anger-In
      (v) Anger-Out
      (vi) State-Anxiety
      (vii) Trait-Anxiety

When you have completed the scoring and calculated your score and level on each of the scales, enter them on the Score and Level Record table below. Then return to the beginning of Chapter 3.

SCORE AND LEVEL RECORD

		Score	Level
(i)	State-Anger	____	____
(ii)	Trait-Anger	____	____
(iii)	Anger-Control	____	____
(iv)	Anger-In	____	____
(v)	Anger-Out	____	____
(vi)	State-Anxiety	____	____
	– non reversed items ____		
	– reversed items ____	____	____
(vii)	Trait-Anxiety	____	____
	– non reversed items ____		
	– reversed items ____	____	____
(viii)	Job-Stress Survey	____	____
	Double-Barrelled Danger	__+__	____

Appendix 1

SELF-ANALYSIS QUESTIONNAIRE STPI FORM X–1

Directions: A number of statements that people use to describe themselves are given below. Read each statement and then circle a number to indicate how you feel *right now*. There are no right or wrong answers. Do not spend too much time on any one statement but give the answer that seems to describe your *present feelings* best.

Ax: S-Anxiety
Ag: S-Anger
(–): Reverse score

			NOT AT ALL	SOMEWHAT	MODERATELY	VERY MUCH	
Ax–	1	I feel calm	1	②	3	4	2
Ag+	2	I am furious	①	2	③	4	3
Ax+	3	I am tense	①	2	3	4	2
Ag+	4	I feel like banging on the table	①	2	3	4	1
Ax–	5	I feel at ease	1	2	③	4	3
Ag+	6	I feel angry	1	②	3	4	2
Ax+	7	I am presently worrying over possible misfortunes	①	2	3	4	1
Ag+	8	I feel like yelling at somebody	①	2	3	4	1
Ax+	9	I feel nervous	①	2	3	4	1
Ag+	10	I feel like breaking things	①	2	3	4	1
Ax+	11	I am jittery	1	②	3	4	2
Ag+	12	I am mad	①	2	③	4	3
Ax–	13	I am relaxed	1	2	③	4	3
Ag+	14	I feel irritated	①	2	③	4	3
Ax+	15	I am worried	1	②	3	4	2
Ag+	16	I feel like hitting someone	①	2	3	4	1
Ax–	17	I feel steady	1	②	3	4	
Ag+	18	I am burned up	1	②	③	4	3
Ax+	19	I feel frightened	①	2	3	4	1
Ag+	20	I feel like swearing	①	2	3	4	1

Copyright © 1979 by C.D. Spielberger. Developed in collaboration with L. Barker, J. Knight, E. Marks, S. Russell, R. Silva de Crane and L. Westberry. Reproduction of this questionnaire by any process without written permission is prohibited.

19

Self-Analysis Questionnaire
STPI Form X–2

Directions: A number of statements that people have used to describe themselves are given below. Read each statement and then circle a number to indicate how you *generally* feel. There are no right or wrong answers. Do not spend too much time on any one statement but give the answer that seems to describe how you *generally* feel.

Ax: T-Anxiety
Ag: T-Anger
(–): Reverse score

Response scale: 1 = Almost Never, 2 = Sometimes, 3 = Often, 4 = Almost Always

Scale	#	Statement	Response
Ax–	21	I am a steady person	1 **(2)** 3 4
Ag+	22	I am quick-tempered	1 2 **(3)** 4
Ax–	23	I feel satisfied with myself	**(1)** 2 3 4
Ag+	24	I have a fiery temper	1 2 **(3)** 4
Ax+	25	I feel nervous and restless	1 2 **(3)** 4
Ag+	26	I am a hotheaded person	1 2 **(3)** 4
Ax+	27	I wish I could be as happy as others seem to be	1 2 **(3)** 4
Ag+	28	I get angry when I'm slowed down by others' mistakes	1 2 **(3)** 4
Ax+	29	I feel like a failure	1 **(2)** 3 4
Ag+	30	I feel annoyed when I am not given recognition for doing good work	1 2 **(3)** 4
Ax+	31	I get in a state of tension or turmoil as I think over my recent concerns and interests	1 2 **(3)** 4
Ag+	32	I fly off the handle	1 2 **(3)** 4
Ax–	33	I feel secure	**(1)** 2 3 4
Ag+	34	When I get mad, I say nasty things	**(1)** 2 3 4
Ax+	35	I lack self-confidence	1 2 3 **(4)**
Ag+	36	It makes me furious when I am criticised in front of others	1 2 3 **(4)**
Ax+	37	I feel inadequate	1 2 3 4
Ag+	38	When I get frustrated, I feel like hitting someone	1 **(2)** 3 4
Ax+	39	I worry too much over something that really does not matter	1 2 **(3)** 4
Ag+	40	I feel infuriated when I do a good job and get a poor evaluation	1 2 **(3)** 4

Copyright © 1979 by C.D. Spielberger. Developed in collaboration with L. Barker, S. Russell, R. Silva de Crane, L. Westberry, J. Knight and E. Marks. Reproduction of this questionnaire by any process without written permission is prohibited.

Appendix 1

ANGER EXPRESSION (AX) SCALE

Directions: Everyone feels angry or furious from time to time, but people differ in the ways that they react when they are angry. A number of statements that people use to describe their reactions when they feel *angry* or *furious* appear below. Read each statement and then circle the number that indicates how *often* you *generally* react or behave in the manner described when you are feeling angry or furious. Remember that there are no right or wrong answers. Do not spend too much time on any one statement.

Rating scale: NOT AT ALL / SOMEWHAT / MODERATELY / VERY MUCH

#	Statement	Response
1	I keep my cool	**(1)** 2 3 4
2	I control my behaviour	**(1)** 2 3 4
3	I control my angry feelings	1 **(2)** 3 4
4	I try to be tolerant and understanding	1 **(2)** 3 4
5	I am patient with others	**(1)** 2 3 4
6	I control my temper	**(1)** 2 3 4
7	I calm down faster than most other people	1 **(2)** 3 4
8	I can stop myself from losing my temper	1 **(2)** 3 4
9	I do things like slam doors	1 **(2)** 3 4
10	I make sarcastic remarks to others	1 **(2)** 3 4
11	I say nasty things	**(1)** 2 3 4
12	If someone annoys me, I tell them how I feel	1 **(2)** 3 4
13	I express my anger	1 2 **(3)** 4
14	I lose my temper	1 2 **(3)** 4
15	I strike out at whatever infuriates me	1 **(2)** 3 4
16	I argue with others	1 2 3 **(4)**
17	I'm irritated much more than people are aware of	1 2 3 **(4)**
18	I boil inside but I don't show it	1 2 3 **(4)**
19	I harbour grudges	1 2 3 **(4)**
20	I am angrier than I am willing to admit	1 2 3 **(4)**
21	I withdraw from people	1 2 3 **(4)**
22	I pout or sulk	1 2 3 **(4)**
23	I am secretly quite critical of others	1 2 3 **(4)**
24	I keep things in	1 2 3 **(4)**

Calculating Your State-Anger Score

As we know, out level of anger is not static. It shifts up and down depending on the situation we are in. We call this emotion State-Anger (S-Anger).

To calculate the S-Anger level that you had at the time you filled in the questionnaires, go back to the Self-Analysis Questionnaire, STPI Form X–1. Ten of the twenty items in this questionnaire measure your S-Anger level. They are marked AG+ in the margin.

The S-Anger items are 2, 4, 6, 8, 10, 12, 14, 16, 18 and 20.

Scoring Make sure you have answered all ten items. For each item, look at the number you have circled. If you have circled a 4 your score for that item is 4; if you circled a 2 your score is 2 for that item. Then simply add up the numbers you have circled for the ten items listed above. The minimum score is 10 and the maximum is 40.

Interpretation of Your S-Anger Score

1 Females use Table A below, males use Table B below.

Table A State-Anger Levels for Females

Level	18–22	Age 23–32	33 or older
Low	–	–	–
Low Average	–	10	10
Average	10–11	11	11–12
High Average	12–15	12–15	13–17
High	16–40	16–40	18–40

Table B State-Anger Levels for Males

Level	18–22	Age 23–32	33 or older
Low	–	–	–
Low Average	10	–	10
Average	11–13	10–11	11
High Average	14–18	12–18	12–14
High	19–40	19–40	15–40

2 Locate the column in the table appropriate for your age and locate your score in that column.
3 Read across to the Level column to find your level of S-Anger. For example, a female aged 26 with a score of 14 would fall in the *High Average* band. A male aged 34 with a score of 18 would fall in the *High* band.

Those with High Average levels probably need to use the suggestions contained in Chapter 4 about how to lower anger levels.

Those with a High level of S-Anger almost certainly have problems with anger. If your Trait-Anger level is also high, immediate attention should be given to changing the beliefs and attitudes that underlie your anger, hostility and aggression.

Calculating Your Trait-Anger Score

Trait-Anger (T-Anger) is a measure of how angry we generally feel. if you are a cool, relaxed and laid-back person most of the time, your level of T-Anger will be low. If you are a fiery, hotheaded person, you will probably get angry in lots of different situations, so you will have a high level of T-Anger. Unlike S-Anger, this is a relatively stable measure, so it won't change much over time unless we make a big effort to change the beliefs and attitudes that underlie all our hostility, anger and aggression.

To calculate your T-Anger level go back to the Self-Analysis Questionnaire STPI Form X–2 in Appendix 1. Locate the 10 items marked AG+ in the margin.

The T-Anger items are numbered 22, 24, 26, 28, 30, 32, 34, 36, 38 and 40.

Scoring

1 Make sure you have answered all the items.
2 Add up your scores on the 10 items listed above counting 4 as 4, 3 as 3 as before. The minimum score is 10 and the maximum is 40.

Interpretation of Your T-Anger Score

1 Females use Table C below. Males use Table D below.

Table C Trait-Anger Levels for Females

Level	Age 18–22	23–32	33 or older
Low	10–15	10–14	10–13
Low Average	16–17	15–16	14–15
Average	18–19	17–18	16–18
High Average	20–23	19–21	19–20
High	24–40	22–40	21–40

Table D Trait-Anger Levels for Males

Level	Age 18–22	23–32	33 or older
Low	10–15	10–14	10–12
Low Average	16–18	15–16	13–14
Average	19–20	17–18	15–16
High Average	21–23	19–21	17–21
High	24–40	22–40	22–40

2 Locate the column in the table appropriate for your age and locate your score in that column.
3 Read across to the Level column to find your level of T-Anger. For example, a female aged 18 with a score of 31 would have a *High* level of T-Anger. A male aged 62 with a score of 12 would have a *Low* level of T-anger.

A High level of T-Anger indicates that you get angry in a wide variety of situations. Almost certainly this is going to cause significant problems in various aspects of your life and you should pay close attention to the material in Chapters 4 and 5, and especially to those sections concerned with changing the attitudes, beliefs and habits that underlie hostility, anger and aggression.

Those with a High Average level probably also need to look carefully at the need to change their behaviour which, from time to time, is bringing them into conflict with those around them.

CALCULATING YOUR EXPRESSION OF ANGER SCORES

The Anger Expression (AX) Scale measures three dimensions.

1. Anger-Control measures the frequency with which we try to control our anger, stop ourselves from losing our temper and try to keep cool.
2. Anger-In measures how often we experience anger but do not express it openly.
3. Anger-Out measures the frequency with which we are likely to express our anger openly and to behave aggressively when we get angry.

Turn now to the Anger Expression Scale in Appendix 1.

A *Calculating Your Anger-Control Score*

Items 1–8 in the AX Scale measure Anger-Control.

Scoring the Anger-Control Sub Scale

Add your scores on the first 8 items of the AX Scale. The minimum score is 8 and the maximum is 32.

Interpretation of Your AX-Control Score

1. Both females and males use Table E.
2. Locate your score in the appropriate column and read across to the Level column to see how your score compares with others of the same gender and of similar age.

Table E Anger-Control Level for Adults

Level	Females	Males
Low	8–18	8–22
Low Average	19–20	23–24
Average	21–23	25–27
High Average	24–26	28–29
High	27–32	30–32

3   The meaning of a Low score is clear. It means that you make little or no attempt to keep your cool and to control your angry feelings. In the two chapters on anger we will argue that this will cause significant problems in various aspects of your life, and that change is desirable.

The meaning of a High score depends on your scores on the Anger-In and Anger-Out measures. Holding anger in seems to lead to elevations in blood pressure and does nothing to solve the problem that caused the anger.

Expressing your anger openly may keep your blood pressure down but it is very likely to alienate those on the receiving end of your aggression. We will argue that the experience of anger can be used positively if we use it as a danger signal, calm down and do something to fix the original problem.

B *Calculating Your Scores on the Anger-In Sub Scale*

Items 17–24 of the AX Scale measure Anger-In.

Scoring the Anger-In Sub Scale

Add up your scores on Items 17–24. The minimum score is 8 and the maximum is 32.

Interpretation of Your Anger-In Score

1   Both males and females use Table F.
2   Locate your score in the appropriate column and read across to find your Anger-In level.

Table F Anger-In Levels for Adults

Level	Females	Males
Low	8 – 11	8 – 11
Low Average	12 – 13	12 – 13
Average	14 – 15	14 – 15
High Average	16 – 18	16 – 18
High	19 – 32	19 – 32

3   A Low or Low Average level indicates that you make little or no attempt to hold your anger in or to keep cool. Sure, you don't boil inside, harbour grudges or sulk, but dumping your anger on others can cause problems.

If you have a High score, you keep your anger inside, withdraw from others and boil inside. This is a recipe for strokes and heart attacks, and you probably need to learn to be more assertive in dealing with others in your environment.

C *Calculating Your Score on the Anger-Out Sub Scale*

Items 9 to 16 of the AX Scale measure Anger-Out.

Scoring the Anger-Out Sub Scale

Add up your scores on Items 9–16. The minimum score is 8 and the maximum is 32.

Interpreting Your Anger-Out Score

1 Both males and females use Table G.
2 Locate your score in the Male or Female columns and read across to find your level on this scale.

Table G Anger-Out Levels for Adults

Level	Females	Males
Low	8–11	8–11
Low Average	12	12
Average	13–14	13–14
High Average	15–17	15–16
High	18–32	17–32

3 A Low score indicates that you do not express your anger openly, strike out or argue with others. Provided you deal with your anger by working out what caused the problem and take some action to deal with it in a calm way, you should cope with life well.

A High or high Average score indicates that you are likely to lose your temper, slam doors and say nasty things. This will almost certainly bring you into conflict with those around you. Dumping your anger on others may keep your blood pressure down but it won't do much for your relationships with others.

CALCULATING YOUR STATE-ANXIETY SCORE

The State-Anxiety (S-Anxiety) Scale measures how anxious you feel at any given point in time. In this case, we have measured your level of anxiety while you were filling in the Self-Analysis Questionnaire STPI Form X–1.

Turn now to the Self-Analysis Questionnaire Form X–1.

Calculating Your S-Anxiety Score

There are ten S-Anxiety items marked either AX+ or AX- in the left-hand margin.

They are numbers 1, 3, 5, 7, 9, 11, 13, 15, 17 and 19.

Items 3, 7, 9, 11, 15 and 19 measure the *presence* of anxiety and are scored in the same way as we scored the anger items, that is, if you have circled a 4 you get a score of 4. If you have circled a 3 you get a score of 3 and so on.

Items 1, 5, 13 and 17 measure the *absence* of anxiety, so we have to reverse the score.

So 1 = 4
    2 = 3
    3 = 2
    4 = 1

Scoring the S-Anxiety Scale

1. Score Items 3, 7, 9, 11, 15 and 19 in the usual way and add up your scores to get a sub-total.
2. Score Items 1, 5, 13 and 17 by reversing the scores and add these up to get a second sub-score.
3. Add the two sub-scores to get your S-Anxiety score.

Interpreting Your S-Anxiety Score

1. Females use Table H and males use Table I.
2. Locate your score in the appropriate Age column.
3. Read across to obtain your Level.

Table H State-Anxiety Levels for Females

Level	18–22	Age 23–32	33 or older
Low	10–12	10–12	10–12
Low Average	13–15	13–15	13–15
Average	16–17	16–18	16–18
High Average	18–23	19–23	19–22
High	24–40	24–40	23–40

Table I State-Anxiety Levels for Males

Level	18–22	Age 23–32	33 or older
Low	10–12	10–13	10–11
Low Average	13–16	14–16	12–14
Average	17–19	17–19	15–17
High Average	20–22	20–21	18–19
High	23–40	22–40	20–40

4 Scores of Low, Low Average and Average indicate little or no problem with anxiety.

A High score indicates your anxiety level is in the top 20 per cent for those of your gender and of approximately your age. You should read the chapters on anxiety very carefully and take steps to reduce your anxiety level.

A High Average level also indicates that the way you react to situations like filling in a questionnaire is a problem for you. If your T-Anxiety level is also high, then you definitely need to do something about your anxiety.

CALCULATING YOUR TRAIT-ANXIETY SCORE

The Trait-Anxiety (T-Anxiety) Scale measures how anxious you generally feel.

Turn now to the Self-Analysis Questionnaire STPI Form X-2.

Calculating Your T-Anxiety Score

There are ten T-Anxiety items marked either AX+ or AX- in the left-hand margin. They are numbers 21, 23, 25, 27, 29, 31, 33, 35, 37 and 39.

Items 25, 27, 29, 31, 35, 37 and 39 measure the *presence* of anxiety and are scored in the usual way. That is, if you have circled a 4 you get a score of 4. If you have circled a 2 you get a score of 2, and so on.

Items 21, 23 and 33 measure the *absence* of anxiety so we have to reverse the scores

    So 1 = 4
         2 = 3
         3 = 2
         4 = 1

Scoring the T-Anxiety Scale

1. Score Items 25, 27, 29, 31, 35, 37 and 39 in the usual way and add up your scores to get a sub-total.
2. Score Items 21, 23 and 33 by reversing the scores and add these up to get a second sub-total.
3. Add the two sub-totals to get your T-Anxiety score.

Interpretation of Your T-Anxiety Score

1. Females use Table J and males use Table K.
2. Locate your T-Anxiety score in the appropriate age column.
3. Read across to the first column to find your level.

Table J Trait-Anxiety Levels for Females

Level	18–22	Age 23–32	33 or older
Low	10–14	10–13	10–12
Low Average	15–17	14–15	13–15
Average	18–19	16–18	16–18
High Average	20–22	19–21	19–22
High	23–40	22–40	23–40

Table K Trait-Anxiety Levels for Males

Level	18–22	Age 23–32	33 or older
Low	10–14	10–13	10–12
Low Average	15–17	14–16	13–14
Average	18–19	17	15
High Average	20–23	18–20	16–18
High	24–40	21–40	19–40

4 A Low or Low Average score means that your T-Anxiety score is in the bottom 40 per cent of those of the same age and gender so anxiety should not be a major problem for you.

Because of the generally high level of anxiety in the community, even an Average T-Anxiety level should be treated seriously. Certainly High Average or High levels indicate that your anxiety will probably cause problems in most areas of your life.

You have now finished scoring these scales. Go back and read Chapters 3 and 4, which describe anger, aggression and hostility, and Chapters 5 and 6, which are about fear, nervousness and anxiety.

appendix 2
JOB-STRESS SURVEY: ARE YOU HASSLED?

Directions: This survey lists ten job-related events that have been identified as stressful by employees working in different settings. Please read each item and circle the number that indicates the approximate number of times during the past month that you have been upset or bothered by each event.

1	I have been bothered by fellow workers not doing their job	0 1 2 3+
2	I've had inadequate support from my supervisor	0 1 2 3+
3	I've had problems getting along with co-workers	0 1 2 3+
4	I've had trouble getting along with my supervisor	0 1 2 3+
5	I've felt pressed to make critical on-the-spot decisions	0 1 2 3+
6	I've been bothered by the fact that there aren't enough people to handle the job	0 1 2 3+
7	I've felt a lack of participation in policy decisions	0 1 2 3+
8	I've been concerned about my inadequate salary	0 1 2 3+
9	I've been trouble by a lack of recognition for good work	0 1 2 3+
10	I've been frustrated by excessive paperwork	0 1 2 3+

Score Yourself: To determine how your stress compares with other workers, add up the points that you circled for each item (0 to 3). Your score will be between 0 and 30. Persons who score between 5 and 8 are about average in how often they experience job-related stress. If you score higher than 9 you may have cause for concern. At 4 or lower you have a relatively non-stressful job. For both males and females, scores of 0 to 4 are Low; scores 5 to 7 are Average; a score of 8 is High Average; and a score of 9 or more is High.

Double-Barrelled Danger: 20+ and 9+.

If you score higher than 20 on Trait-Anger in Appendix 1 and if your score is higher than 9 on the Job-Stress Survey, you've got a dangerous combination going. Better cool yourself or the job. Double-digit job-stress points to trouble, especially if your personality runs high in irritability and temper. Remember the double-barrelled effect. If your personality makes you anger-prone, watch out for jobs high in petty aggravations. On the Score and Level Record, scores of 20+ and 9+ are High. All others are Average.

Enter your scores and levels in the Score and Level Record and then return to page 38 and read on.

references

Friedman, M., 1974. *Type A Behavior and Your Heart.* Fawcett, Greenwich.

Friedman, M. and Ulmer, R.N., 1984. *Treating Type A Behavior and Your Heart.* Alfred Knopf, New York.

Gaudry, E., 1990. *Your Must Give in to Win.* Collins Dove, Melbourne

Gaudry, E. and Spielberger, C.D., 1971. *Anxiety and Educational Achievement.* John Wiley and Sons, Sydney.

Gordon, T., 1955. *Group-Centred Leadership.* Houghton-Mifflin, Boston.

Johnson, E. H., 1984. 'Anger and anxiety as determinants of elevated blood pressure in adolescents'. Unpublished doctoral dissertation. University of South Florida, Tampa.

Rogers, C.R., 1969. *Freedom to Learn.* C.E. Merril, Columbus.

Spielberger, C.D. (ed), 1966. *Anxiety and Behavior.* Academic Press, New York.

Spielberger, C. D., 'Anxiety as an emotional state'. In Spielberger, C. D. (ed), 1972. *Anxiety: Current Trends in Theory and Research.* Vol. 1, Academic Press, New York.

Spielberger, C.D., 1983. *Manual for State-Trait Anxiety Inventory.* Consulting Psychologists Press, Palo Alto.

Spielberger, C.D., Jacobs, G., Russell, S. and Crane, R.S., 1983. 'Assessment of Anger: The State-Trait Anger Scale'. In Butcher, J.N. and Spielberger, C.D. (eds), 1983. *Advances in Personality Assessment.* Vol. 2, Lea, Hillsdale.

Spielberger, C.D., Jacobs, G., Crane, R.S., Russell, S., Westberry, L., Barker, L., Johnson, E., Knight, J. and Marks, E., 1979. *Preliminary Manual for the State-Trait Personality Inventory (STPI).* University of South Florida Human Resources Institute.

Spielberger, C.D., Krasner, S.S. and Solomon, E.P., 1988. 'The Experience, Expression and Control of Anger'. In Janisse, M.P. (ed.), *Health Psychology: Individual Differences and Stress.* Springer Verlag, New York.

Spielberger, C.D., and London, P., 1982. Rage Boomerangs: Lethal Type A Anger. *American Health.* Vol. 1, pp. 52–6.

The Self Alone

I recommend *The Self Alone* as an insightful and thought-provoking book and a potential classic. It is not only the most complete collection of insights on the subject of loneliness I have ever read, it is also a positive and uplifting read — for every issue raised, there is a suggestion which will improve the reader's mental and physical wellbeing.

PAMELA ALLARDICE, Editor
Nature & Health magazine

Loneliness is something we have all experienced, however fleetingly, in our lives. But are some of us more prone to feelings of loneliness than others? How do our early experiences affect our ability to cope with being alone in adult life?

The Self Alone explores the meaning of loneliness and provides insights into the experience. It encourages a shift in the way we view loneliness, helping us to use it to transform our lives.

Angela Rossmanith is a freelance writer and contributing editor in the areas of health, social issues and personal relationships.

CollinsDove
An imprint of HarperCollins*Publishers*

ISBN 1863714480

Think like a shrink

Have you ever wondered...
What's wrong with me?
What's wrong with my children?
Am I going **mad**?
... then perhaps this book is for you.

In *Think like a shrink* Dr Joseph Dunn takes us behind the scenes of his busy psychiatric practice and shows us 'warts and all' how this psychiatrist thinks. Using case studies based on practical experience, he introduces us to some of the things that go wrong in our lives and to some of the ways in which psychiatry can help us fix them. He also includes a chapter on finding a therapist to suit our needs and personality.

In his own humorous, original way, Dr Dunn reveals that his profession is a helping, caring one and that psychiatrists are, after all, human.

Before beginning his training in psychiatry, **Dr Joseph Dunn** acquired extensive experience in obstetrics, general practice and occupational medicine. Now, as a Fellow of the Royal Australian College of Psychiatry, he feels he has finally found his niche.

CollinsDove
An imprint of HarperCollins*Publishers*

ISBN 1863713840